Cross and Mission

Challenges and Priorities in Evangelisation Among the Indigenous People of North India

Cross and Mission

Challenges and Priorities in Evangelisation Among the Indigenous People of North India

Paul Chungath

2010

Cross and Mission : Challenges and Priorities in Evangelisation Among the Indigenous People of North India — published by the Rev. Dr. Ashish Amos of Indian Society for Promoting Christian Knowledge (ISPCK), Post Box 1585, 1654, Madarsa Road, Kashmere Gate, Delhi-110006.

ISBN: 978-81-8465-117-1

Cover Design: Bro. Sijo Chungath

Laser typeset by

ISPCK, Post Box 1585, 1654, Madarsa Road, Kashmere Gate, Delhi-110006 • *Tel:* 23866323

e-mail: ashish@ispck.org.in • ella@ispck.org.in
website: www.ispck.org.in

Dedicated to

All Missionaries of Sagar Diocese

Contents

Acknowledgements

I am grateful to Most Rev Leo Cornelio SVD, Archbishop of Bhopal, for his foreword to this book and Most Rev. Anthony Chirayath, Bishop of Sagar, for his encouragements in my ministry and comments on the back cover of this book. I express my sincere gratitude to Prof. Ruth Henderson and Rev. Sr. Philippa CSSJ for reviewing this work. I acknowledge with gratitude ISPCK, Delhi, for their readiness to publish this book.

Foreword

The recent atrocities against Christians in different parts of our country make us realise that we need to review our methods of carrying out the mission of the Lord and being at the service of the people. In spite of these atrocities, evangelisation continues to be our central and primordial concern, so all our activities should contribute to this cause. I am sure that we will find many creative ways of venturing into this evangelising mission. But in our effort to find new and creative ways of evangelisation, we should not forget the essentially best method of witnessing to the word and of facing challenges of carrying the cross as a true follower of the Lord.

The cross in an essential part of the mission for a believer in Christ, more so for a missionary. There is no mission without the cross. A missionary cannot eliminate the cross from his or her mission work. That is very clear from the life of Jesus himself. A missionary who is unwilling to carry the cross cannot be a true disciple of Christ.

With the Vatican II, mission itself took a different connotation and everyone involved in mission work propagated the axiom 'Church is a mission' not 'Church has a mission.' This is confirmed by the Church documents that say 'Church is missionary by her very nature' (AG #2) or 'Church exists to evangelise the world which is her essential function, identity and vocation' (EN #14). Though traditionally the Church's mission was meant for those who did not know Christ (evangelising the unevangelised), with time, mission was extended to those who knew Christ insufficiently. Mission today includes also re-evangelising the already evangelised.

Today, the need is to witness the Gospel in our lives, or rather, our life should be 'the gospel' we proclaim. Pope John Paul II in *Redemptoris Missio* says, "People today put more trust in witnesses than in teachers, in experience than in teaching and in life and action than in theories. The witness of a Christian life is the first and irreplaceable form of mission" (RM # 42). Today, people, especially people of other faiths, may not have read the Bible but Christians and missionaries may be the only Bible they may read. That is why Archbishop Oscar Romerro said that we must preach the Word of God wherever we go, but sometimes we will have to use the words. This needs an ongoing *kenosis* by missionaries, which is both a challenge and a cross.

Today, in India, mission is primarily not so much converting to Christianity as the conversion of heart and change of attitude. Traditionally, mission, in India has been carried out through education, health care, social and developmental activities, etc., and the Church, through these activities, tries to reach out to the poor, rural, dalit, tribal/indigenous people. The challenges missionaries encounter are the daily crosses that every follower of Jesus has to face as Jesus himself said, "If they have persecuted me they will persecute you too" (Jn 15:20). This evangelising mission is, of course, often criticised by the fundamentalists as a ploy for conversion. Though their accusations are baseless, the Church faces them in good faith and for the sake of the Lord. This, indeed, is the self-denial that Jesus speaks of when he says, "If any man would come after me, let him deny himself and take up his cross and follow me" (Mth 16:24). God does not take away the cross from our mission but makes the burden (cross) light.

Evangelisation needs to take into consideration the specific culture, which is a complex reality. The evangeliser has to be sensitive to the culture of a particular society or group. When we involve ourselves in the evangelising mission among the indigenous people of North India, we need to pay utmost attention to the customs and cultural elements of the people. Living in the changing multi-religious, socio-economic and political reality of India, missionaries need to be incarnated in the life-situation of people. The language of the people, whom we evangelise, should be the medium of communication for better evangelisation.

Fr. Paul Chungath has done a fine job of convincing the reader or missionary that challenges and crosses are part and parcel of our evangelising mission. He has developed the theme in the North-Indian framework, thus making it contextualised and relevant to the local setting and present times. The author, who himself works among tribals and dalits, knows their plight and their needs. He has described many pastoral challenges faced by the missionaries and proposed several missionary priorities in view of making our mission more relevant among the indigenous people of North India. Some of the priorities that the author has proposed are worth remembering, namely need for adequate formation of would-be missionaries, encouraging local vocations and lay missionaries and evangelising through inculturation.

I hope this book will inspire all missionaries, especially priests and religious and lay leaders, involved in evangelising mission among the tribals and dalit people of North India.

+Leo Cornelio SVD
Archbishop of Bhopal

Introduction

The call to follow the path of Jesus and be a missionary for Christ includes carrying the cross. Jesus said, "If any man would come after me, let him deny himself and take up his cross and follow me" (Mt. 16:24; Mk. 8:34; Lk. 9:23). On another occasion, again, Jesus emphasised that the criterion to be a worthy follower of Christ is the ability to carry one's own daily cross (cf. Mt. 10:38; Lk. 14:27). While sending the disciples for ministry Jesus cautioned about the future sufferings they would have to face because of being his disciples (cf. Mt. 10-16-25). Jesus also taught that the good results of an evangeliser depend on the measure he gives up his life for the sake of the Gospel: "Unless a grain of wheat falls into the earth and dies, it remains alone; but if it dies, it bears much fruit" (Jn.12:24). These teachings of Jesus highlight that the cross or hardships are in the nature of missionary vocation and the success of a missionary depends on his or her readiness to lose his or her life for the sake of Gospel. Jesus encouraged us to go ahead with courage even in the midst of persecutions (cf. Mt. 10:26-31), and these consoling words of Jesus can be an inspirational force in the present situation in India.

'Mission' is the term usually given to those particular undertakings by which the heralds of the Gospel are sent by the Church into the world to carry out the task of preaching the Gospel and implanting the Church among peoples who are non-believers in Christ.[1] Evangelisation is considered to be the fundamental duty of the people of God and according to canon Law all Christ's faithful must be conscious of the responsibility to play their part in missionary activity (Canon 781). India is a country with a vast majority of people of other faiths, which counts up to around 98 per cent. The missionary command of Christ and the teachings of the Church on the important duty of Christian faithful in the field of Evangelisation is the underlying inspiration for this book. As Indian Church history shows, tribals in India are quite receptive to the Gospel message. The missionary success in the Chottanagpur area is one of the living examples. At present, evangelisation among the tribal communities in India faces many challenges. The theme of this book, thus, finds its roots in the present situation.

Recently, missionaries in India underwent a crucial time due to persecutions from fanatical Hindu organisations, which have also affected evangelisation among tribals in India. It is not an all-of-a-sudden happening. Various forms of persecutions were happening since half a century. And it continues in different part of India though not as seriously as it happened in Orissa during 2007-2009. Thus, we are in a period where evangelisation has become rather difficult; the time has come to evaluate our traditional methods considering the contemporary world and search for new methods for effective mission in the modern-day society.

The progress of humanity at various levels has an effect in the receptivity of religion. There are many reasons for the new situation of society: educational development, change of lifestyle, new organisations in various religions to strengthen

---

[1] *Ad Gentes Divinitus,* Decree on the Church's Missionary Activity (7 December 1965) 6.

one's own religion, politicisation of religion, growth of secularism and communistic thought pattern. Ignoring the contemporary situation of the society and retaining old methods, a missionary may end up with unpleasant results. As it was stated by S. Fuchs, "A missionary's message of peace may lead to strife and bloodshed; his preaching of a pure doctrine may lead to ecstatic madness."[2] Thus, the means of evangelisation must be most suitable and effective for communicating the Gospel message to the people of our times.[3]

This book focuses on the concrete situations of today, the problems that a missionary has to face in order to bring fruits in his missionary endeavours. Contemporary challenges in the field of evangelisation among the North Indian tribes leading to essential measures in the form of proposed priorities are seen in the framework of this book. The various definitions of evangelisation reflect different characteristics; and one of them has been given by J. Dinh Duc Dao: "Missonary Evangelisation is a complex reality that involves different aspects: preaching and witnessing to the Gospel, working together with those who seek justice and peace, and again: sharing, inculturation, reciprocal enrichment with other Christians, dialogue with believers of all religions."[4]

The contemporary evangelisation among the tribals is dealt with in two dimensions: challenges and priorities. Evangelisation among tribals in North India is facing great trials, and various atrocities have occurred against Christians,

---

[2] S. FUCHS, *Anthropology for the Missions*, St. Paul Publications, Allahabad 1979, 116.

[3] Paul VI, Apostolic Exhortation, *Evangelii Nuntiandi* (8 December 1975) 40.

[4] J. Dinh Duc Dao, "Missiography: Present Situations and Emerging Tendencies of Mission," in *Correspondence Course on Missionary Formation: Mission for the Third Millennium*, Pontifical Missionary Union, Roma 1991, 14.

especially the missionaries. The first part of the book covers the external and internal challenges that evangelisation faces today. The second part of this book consists of a section of priorities for better evangelisation among the tribals of North India. The basis for these priorities is established in the first part of this book in the light of analysis from the challenges presented. These priorities are in a way a proposal for better evangelisation in the light of challenges and recent magisterial teachings of the Church.

The first chapter deals with the ever-growing religious fundamentalism in North India that creates challenging obstacles in the way of evangelisation. This phenomenon is seen under four subtitles: fundamentalist organisations against religious freedom, accusation of conversion, attacks from Hindu fundamentalist organisations and re-conversion.

The second chapter is a study offered on the challenges from the accusation of detribalisation by Christian missionaries through their missionary activities. There are mainly three levels of accusations against Christian missionaries in relation to detribalisation: religious practices of tribals, a new lifestyle affecting tribal unity and solidarity and their indigenous art and language. How Christian missionaries are causing the above-mentioned levels of detribalisation according to the accusers is seen in this chapter.

There are also certain internal factors that become the cause for inefficiency in the missionary proclamation; consequently, missionary activities are not able to achieve the goal in the way expected. These elements are also seen as challenges in this book. These challenges are termed as challenges from the incongruity of missionaries. There are three major elements that become a real challenge for the contemporary missionary proclamation: Insufficiency of deep-rootedness in local culture and in one's own faith, defects in the formation and insufficiency of incarnated and solidarity – forwarded movement. The third chapter deals with these challenges.

From the fourth chapter onwards, the proposed priorities for better results in evangelisation are covered. Chapter 4 focuses on the adequate and appropriate formation of missionaries. Firstly, the need is re-orientation of present missionaries to face the present external challenges. Secondly, promotion of local vocations and lay missionaries are considered as the thrust. The third element of consideration in this chapter is the urgent need of contextual and tribal theology in formation houses.

The witnessing of Gospel values are considered as an important need for missionary proclamation. And this aspect is the theme for the fifth chapter. The people of today accept more the exemplary life of a person than mere words preached. Life witness of missionary has a vital role to play in effectiveness of this missionary activity. Therefore, this aspect is taken as the first consideration in this chapter. In general, North-Indian tribals are economically poor and undergoing various exploitations from wealthier groups. Thus, prophetic witness and work for liberation is another field of action considered as an essential need in the evangelisation among North-Indian tribal communities. This is the second sub heading in this chapter. Economical backwardness of these indigenous people opens another aspect of witnessing, namely charitable services. Thus, promotion of Christian values through witnessing of charity is the final aspect dealt with in this chapter.

The sixth chapter is based on the plurality of religious and cultural situation of India with special emphasis on the different tribal communities in the country. There are various elements to be considered in this particular context of cultural plurality. Therefore, we are having three main subtitles as priorities: healthy relations with local religions and inculturation, promotion of tribal culture through tribalisation movements and tribal identity and mission.

The final chapter deals with the priority in primacy of proclamation.Proclamation of the Word of God is the obligation and duty of each and every Christian. This may be done through word or deed with prudence according to the situation of each place. Obstacles and persecution are not an excuse to abstain from this duty. For convenience, this priority in relation with the proclamation is divided under three subtitles: primacy of proclamation as a commitment, primacy of proclamation to the tribals and proclamation with renewed spirit and courage.

CHAPTER 1
Challenges from Religious Fundamentalism

Christian tribals in North India confronted attacks from fundamentalists on several occasions in this decade, and a peaceful atmosphere for evangelisation is a distant hope of the future. Missionaries who work among the tribes are on the hit list of Hindu fundamentalist organisations, and occasional disturbances have now become a normal case. The extreme form of these attacks was experienced recently in Orissa, and normality has not yet been regained for the tribal people who fled to the forest. The process of peace and re-settling the Christian tribals in their villages is going on.

Religious fundamentalism is a burning issue. It challenges evangelisation among the tribals in North India. We will analyse it in four dimensions in this chapter: fundamentalist organisations against religious freedom, accusations regarding conversions, attacks from fundamentalist organisations and the re-conversion process led by Hindu fundamentalist organisations.

Fundamentalist Organisations Against Religious Freedom

The escalation of tensions between the Muslim world and the West, terrorist activities sponsored by religious sectarian groups in India, Asia and elsewhere and the revival of many sects with a fundamentalist tendency within living religions and cultures stand witness to rising religious fundamentalism. Some political leaders consider the tribal resistance movements in India as movements instigated by western Christians. Prohibition of religious freedom and the state-sponsored religious terrorism testify to this reality.[1]

The challenge arises out of the contemporary context, and that has to do with increasing religious fundamentalism. Religious fundamentalism poses a significant problem to the cause of mission and evangelisation among the tribes in India. For example, since its inception the *Rashtriya Swayamsewak Sangh* (RSS) has promoted the politicised religious ideology known as *Hindutva*, which is shared also by the *Vishwa Hindu Parishad* and *Bajrang Dal*, who do not want to affirm the legitimacy of non-Hindu minorities like the Muslims and Christians in India. The *Hindutva* ideology claims for Indians one (Hindu) nation, one (Hindu) culture and one (Hindu) state. Recently, these forms of fundamentalism have been intensified and there have been more atrocities against

---

[1] Cf. W. Longchar, "Tribal Theology in the Changing Context," in *Religion and Society*, 52, 3-4 (2007), 93-94. "Because of the identification of religion with one's own culture and with the social identity of the group, the Asian could be very tolerant and at the same time intransigent and fanatical with regard to religion. He is tolerant towards the religion of others but becomes intransigent and fanatical when it is a question of his own religion, particularly when it seems to be threatened. . . . So long as religion is considered as an element of the culture that constitutes the social identity of the group, and particularly if it is supported by a political power, there will not only be little possibility of Evangelisation, but inner freedom to follow the light of the truth will also be very limited" (J. DINH DUC DAO, "Evangelisation and Culture in Asia: Problems and Prospects," in *Omnis Terra* 28, Eng. ed., 1994, 76).

Christians in the past ten years than in the preceding fifty years. This means that Christians have to respond to the challenges of these forms of fundamentalism primarily from an ideological perspective.[2] This great challenge demands from us answers to some difficult questions: What is the role of the Church? How can she become relevant and effective, especially from the perspective of evangelisation? At the same time, against the *Hindutva* background, what could be the meaning of evangelisation today? P. C. Mehta explains how this challenge has affected the mission among the Bhils:

> The emergence of Christianity and conversion of Bhils invited the reactions of Arya Samaj during pre-independence days and Vishwa Hindu Parishad after Independence. However, these two organizations could not break much ice and they mainly concentrated on converting the Bhils. Vishwa Hindu Parishad is still working and concentrates on countering Christianity. Their main aim is to bring tribals into the Hindu fold.[3]

As far as the process of inculturation is concerned, the Bhagat movement has done enough to attack the identity of Bhils and has tried to convert them into the fold of Hindus. It is

---

[2] Cf. A. Aghamkar, "Contemporary Mission Challenges in India," in *Dharma Deepika*, 9, 2 (2005), 75.

[3] P. C. Mehta, *Changing Face of Bhils*, Shiva Publishers, Udaipur 1998, 127. The chief object of the Arya Samaj, founded by Dayandanda Saraswathi in 1875, was to bring about social and religious revival through the renaissance of early Hindu doctrine, its favourite mottoes being 'Back to the Vedas' and 'Aryavarta for the Aryans' (Smith, 1938:57). This view simply equated Indian culture with Hinduism and Hindu culture; all non-Hindu aspects were regarded as contaminating influences. These views are the basis from which later Hindu movements and organisations such as the Hindu Mahasabha, R.S.S., Shiva Sena, VHP, Bajarang Dal and BJP are formed (S. M. Michael, "Real Issues behind the Violence," in *Mission Today*, 2, (2000), 12).

very difficult to say that they have been Hinduised, as there are traits that provide them a separate identity. This has also raised the question of their identity and their integration with the rest of the society. The Hindu society has not accepted them as part of their social stratification, although Hindu organisations like Vishwa Hindu Parishad and even some anthropologists and sociologists have considered them backward Hindus. But after reviewing the structural features of both the communities, one can say that the case is not such, while Christians believe that they are tribals. Hindu organisations are, in fact, training them by Sanskritising Hindu traits. A training School for Bhils has been opened where young tribals are trained. This is the creation of the Brahmin caste among the Bhils.[4]

The *Hindutva* ideology of fundamentalist organisations does not recognise the plurality of Indian cultures and religions; above all, this ideology rejects the fundamental constitutional rights that Indians do have religious freedom and they should enjoy it well. This ideology should not be allowed to harm the basic virtues of freedom and social harmony in India. Secondly, Christians should respond to the challenges of fundamentalism from a practical perspective: They should be well-informed about the ideological intentions and practical methods used by the fundamentalists. They should approach the law-enforcement authorities to guarantee and maintain religious freedom and social harmony. Thus, Christians must be prepared to respond to the challenge of *Hindutva* in a more assertive and balanced way. Christian organisations such as the All India Christian Council provide a common forum to address various issues related to *Hindutva* and other forms of religious fundamentalism.[5]

---

[4] Cf. P. C. Mehta, *Changing Face of Bhils*, 128.

[5] Cf. A. Aghamkar, "Contemporary Mission Challenges in India," 75.

During the past two decades, Hinduism has become a world phenomenon. Its *pracharaks* and preachers are working overtime both in the country and abroad to spread the Hindu religion, philosophy, culture and spirituality. In India, it has taken an aggressive turn in recent times. Mobilisation of the Hindu masses with various types of *Yatras* is one of the strategies. Construction of temples at every prominent avenue or boulevard in all cities and towns is another.[6]

By taking out religious processions through the streets on various occasions, flaunting weapons in their hands, violent Hindu elements are demonstrating that they can flex their muscles in the name of religion. Indirectly, the message of intimidation and subjugation is sent to minority communities every now and then. There is also the explicitly violent outfit called Bajrang Dal. In many cities of North India, there is a parallel administration by these fundamentalist organisations. They are capable of organising attacks instantly as their foot soldiers are well equipped with the latest gadgets of communication and means of transportation.[7]

Accusation of Conversion

The term *conversion* is understood differently in Christian theology and in the Indian context, especially among Hindu fundamentalist organisations. In the Christian theological context, *conversion* would mean change of heart (*metanoia*), but Hindu fundamentalists would take this term as changing of

---

[6] Cf. A. Poruthur, "Contemporary Challenges for Mission in North India," in *Mission Today*, 10, 4 (2008), 358.

[7] Cf. *ibid.*, 359. In an attack on the novices of Presentation Sisters near Bhopal (15 May 2008), some 30 young men descended on the scene within no time.

religion or proselytising.[8] The Synoptic Gospels portray both John the Baptist and Jesus as preachers of repentance (Gk *metanoia*). Jesus' preaching is a call for repentance (Mk. 1:15; Mt. 4:17), and Jesus' parables reveal an implicit understanding that repentance involves a converted or transformed understanding of God. The content of John's preaching was with the prophetic motif of repentance and return to God.[9] Hindu fundamentalists in India directly go for only one meaning for the term *conversion*, namely change of religion with persuasion. The conversion issue is the major accusation against Christianity in India and has often resulted in violence against Christians and institutions owned by them.

According to the observation of H. C. Upreti, Christian missionaries gave economic allurement to the tribal people and thus persuaded some of the tribals to embrace Christianity. This, at several places, divided tribals into two segments – Christian tribals and non-Christian tribals. The problem arises when one section opposes such a move, as it recently happened in Gujarat, Orissa and elsewhere, when religious conversion created problems.[10] The conversion issue did a lot of damage

---

[8] One set of meanings for the word conversion given by the Oxford Dictionary: "The action of converting, or fact or being converted, to religion, a belief, or opinion; *spec.* to Christianity. 2. *Theol.* The turning of sinners to God; a spiritual change from sinfulness to a religious life" (W Little – H.W. Fowler – J. Coulson, "Conversion" in *The Shorter Oxford English Dictionary*, Oxford University Press, London 1944, 387).

[9] B. R. Gaventa, "Conversion," in D. N. Freedman, *The Anchor Bible Dictionary*, Vol. 1, Doubleday, New York 1992, 1132.

[10] Cf. H. C. Upreti, *Indian Tribes: Then and Now*, Pointer Publishers, Jaipur 2007, 206. A headline in *The Statesman* of November 4, 1970, proclaimed 'Rajasthan Bill to Check Conversion' :"To put an end to forcible conversions of Scheduled Castes and Scheduled Tribes, a Bill–Rajasthan Freedom of Religions Bill

to evangelisation in India. Every humanitarian service of Christian missionaries is seen from this point of view:

> VHP's Ashok Singhal argues that Professor Amartya Sen's Nobel Prize is a Christian conspiracy to open more missionary run educational institutions to convert the poor. It was alleged that missionaries use force, fraud and allurements to convert people to Christianity. Funds obtained for welfare activities are used for conversion.[11]

Many of the indigenous people came into contact with Christianity when colonial powers entered and overran the lands in which they lived. Some propagandists led the Indians to believe that colonial powers have been purposefully instrumental in the entry of Christianity into various Asian countries. Thus, attempts are being made to link colonialism with the spread of Christianity. This is fraught with many problems. In Asian countries, where the majority non-indigenous portion of the population is not Christian, it is suspected that Christianity divided and continues to divide

---

1970–was introduced in the State Assembly today. The Bill seeks to prohibit conversion from one religion to another by use of force or by fraudulent means, to impose effective curb on conversion of poor and uneducated people" (J. F. SEUNARINE, *Reconversion to Hinduism through Suddhi*, The Christian Literature Society, Madras 1977, 81- 82).

[11] S. M. Michael, "Real Issues Behind the Violence," 15. "With regard to movements to Christianity, several Hindu fundamentalists accuse that there were forceful conversions in the last 500 years. Studied on conversion movements indicate that this is a much more complicated problem. Firstly, we have to assess different historical periods and varied political regimes and the accounts are not the same for each. Further, the idea that missionaries came with the sword to convert, i.e., they have always had the backing of the colonial state and the power to use military force to enforce conversions is seriously challenged by the historical data" (*ibid.*, 17).

the indigenous peoples from the "mainstream" majority group or population.[12]

However, the major accusation against Christian missionaries is that they are converting Hindus to Christianity, but this is not true when we analyse concretely various attacks against the Christians. In the present situation, one can easily understand that the reasons behind the attacks on Christian missionaries by various Hindu nationalist organisations are not mainly because of the conversion issue but political motives and the vested interest in subjugating the poor. These two motives are seen behind most of the violence against Christian missionaries in India. The observation of S. M. Michael is worth recalling; he states:

> The work of Christian missionaries among the downtrodden people of this country will go against the interest of the upper castes. That is why Pastor Rev. Graham Stewart Staines, who was working among the lepers in a remote part of Orissa, was burned to death. The nuns who are working in the remotest parts of India are raped. Christian educational and social institutions are ransacked and missionaries humiliated.[13]

---

[12] Cf. D. Jala, "What the Church can do with/for Indigenous Peoples," in M. SATURNINO DIAS, *Indigenous Peoples in Asia and Challenges of the Future*, Claretian Publications, Bangalore 2004, 49. See the writing of A. Shouri, *Harvesting Our Souls: Missionaries, Their Design, Their Claims*, ASA Publications, New Delhi, 2000.

[13] S. M. Michael, "Real Issues Behind the Violence,"14. A similar statement was made by Archbishop Alan De Lastic: "Christian educational and developmental organizations are victims of violence, together with priests and preachers. These institutions are targeted because they are sensitizing and empowering the people, particularly those who have been exploited and subjugated." Archbishop Alan De Lastic, "Violations of Human Rights and Attack on Christians", *Supplement to Indian Currents*, 10, 48 (1998) 36.

Though there are accusations against Christian missionaries about forcible conversion, the number of Christians in India has not gone high. As it was rightly remarked, "In spite of the conversions that took place during more than two hundred years of British Raj and fifty years thereafter the Christian community still numbers under 3% of our population."[14]

Attacks from Fundamentalist Organisations

The Indian Church is now undergoing a crucial period due to the violence against tribal Christians and missionaries in Orissa. This violence is spreading slowly to other parts of India. Jhabua Bhil Christians and missionaries have been the victims of attacks from Hindu fanatics for many years and now the terror has increased, as it has spread all over India. These attacks create terror among the tribals who wish to embrace Christianity and put obstacles in the way of evangelisation.

The emerging scenario is one of intensification of persecution of Christians. According to the statistics available from the All India Christian council, there have been at least 250 verified and documented incidents so far, excluding the recent attacks in Orissa.[15] It may be good to refresh our memory with some of the major atrocities committed against Christians, like those in the Dangs district (Gujarat) in 1998 and the killing of Graham Staines and his two little children.[16]

---

[14] J. Saldana, "Conversion in 'Ecclesia in Asia'," in *Mission Today*, 2, 2 (2000) 174.

[15] Cf. A. Poruthur, "Contemporary Challenges for Mission in North India," 355; cf. J. DAYAL, "A Book in Saffron Language," *Indian Currents*, 21-27 (2008), Delhi, 33.

[16] Cf. A. Poruthur, "Contemporary Challenges for Mission in North India," 355.

Mr. Staines, who had worked for 34 years with Indian lepers, was killed on 23rd January 1999 by Hindu extremists. This incident was reported in the press:

> The police blamed members of a Hindu extremist group, *Bajarang Dal*, for killing Graham Staines, 58, and his two boys on Saturday in the eastern state of Orissa after setting on fire the jeep in which they slept.[17]

There were several attacks on the missionaries who are involved in the evangelisation service among the Bhils in Jhabua. One such acts of violence took the form of a gang rape of four nuns in the Jhabua district of Madhya Pradesh. This type of violence against the Christian community has not ended.[18] In the opinion of S. M. Michael, there is a pattern in attacks against the Christian community in India. This can be seen in the several fact-finding reports given by non-governmental organisers. The major fact that emerges from these investigations is that communal riots and the rise of the Sangh Parivar go hand in hand. This is clear from the statements of the investigating officials and the leaders.[19] A

---

[17] "India Vows to Punish Christians' Murderers," in *International Herald Tribune*, Tuesday, (January 26, 1999), 6.

[18] Cf. A. De Lastic, Archbishop, "Address at the Press Conference by the Chairman of the United Christian Forum for Human Rights on 24th November 1998," in *Supplement to Indian Currents*, 10, 48 (1998) 40-42.

[19] Cf. S. M. Michael, "Real Issues Behind the Violence," 9-10. S. M. Michael's opinion derived from these reports: *"Then They Came for the Christians – A Report to the Nation"* by AIFOFDR, 1999; *Report of the United Christians' Forum for Human Rights* (UCFHR) 1999; *Violence in Gujarat – Hindu Jago Christi Bhago* by Kamal Mitra for National Alliance of Women, 1999 (*ibid.* 9). Another basis for this affirmation is following statements of officials quoted by S. M. Michael in his article, "The DGP (Director General of Police) of Gujarat where the attacks on Christians were in large scale, said: 'The VHP and the Bajrang Dal were

member of the investigation team sent by the Minorities Commission is again affirming this fact: "After initial reluctance, the officials named VHP and Bajarang Dal allegedly involved in the mob attacks on Christians and Muslims."[20] The Bhils of Jhabua were also attacked by Hindu fundamentalist organisations, and in Orissa violence against tribal Christians is still going on:

> In 2004 Christians were attacked in several places in the Jhabua district of Madhya Pradesh. Still fresh in our minds is what happened in Orissa on Christmas Day 2007 and the following days during which about 5,000 people were terrorized and displaced. Obviously North India is becoming increasingly intolerant towards Christians and other minorities.[21]

The recent Hindu extremist violence against tribal Christians and missionaries in Orissa, which started on 24th August 2008, has continued almost unabated since then. At least 50 Christians have been murdered, some cut to pieces and others burnt alive. Many feared that the death toll is even higher, with one estimate suggesting that 120 Christians have been killed. About 18,000 people have been injured, many of them severely; numerous Christian women have been raped; some 4,400 homes have been destroyed; 300 villages have been cleansed of all Christians, and several orphanages and hundreds of Churches and Church buildings have been

---

taking the law into their own hands" (*The Hindustan Times,* August 6, 1998). This is also confirmed by the Archbishop of Delhi, Alan de Lastic, who said: "What I have noticed is that ever since this Government came to power at the Centre, the attacks on Christians and Christian missionaries have increased." (see *Frontline,* 1993: 123); (*ibid.,*10).

[20] *The Indian Express,* August 12, 1998.

[21] A. Poruthur, "Contemporary Challenges for Mission in North India," 356.

torched and razed. Relief camps, where Christians have fled for safety and shelter, have been attacked and drinking water has been poisoned. Over 50, 000 Christians are thought to be homeless and around 30,000, more than half of them children, were hiding in the jungle, many without any food and water. Starvation was a very real danger for many of them, especially for the children, the elderly and the sick.[22]

Hindu fundamentalist organisations already set a price for those who kill Christians. The highest price, 250 dollars, is for those who kill a Catholic priest or a pastor who is involved in the mission of evangelisation.[23] These reports show how hard it will be for future evangelisation in India, especially among tribals of North India.

Hindutva fundamentalist organisations are after ethnic cleansing. One of the fundamentalist groups that attacked FCC sisters in Indore (M. P.) in October 2007 started with threats to get them out of the place. Besides these virulent fanatics, there are many sympathisers as well. There is another large section of passive people. Though there are some who are fully committed to the ideal of secularism, their voice has limited reach among the mainline Hindus.[24]

Re-conversion (*Ghar Vapsi*)

When the British introduced the system of taking the census of the country they used religious categories along with another section called 'Animists' which stood for the tribals.

---

[22] Cf. N. Scavo, "Il cuore di Milano per i cristiani dell'India", in *Avenire* (23 Novembre 2008), 27; cf. S. Vecchia, "Orissa, il drama di mogli e madri" in *Avenire* (14 Dicembre 2008), 1,5.

[23] Cf. s. n. "In India premi dagli estremisiti indù a chi uccide cattolici", in *Avenire* (23 Novembre 2008), 3.

[24] Cf. A. Poruthur, "Contemporary Challenges for Mission in North India," 365.

Already in 1951, with the first census of independent India, that latter category was removed and those who had not embraced one of the formal religions were automatically co-opted into the Hindu fold. As the leaders of the tribes have not woken up to this census fraud, the practice continues even now. An eminent sociologist like M. N. Srinivas with his upper caste background and mentality also subscribed to the same view of including tribals as Hindus. Another renowned sociologist, T. K. Oommen, tried to draw the attention of Srinivas to the fact that tribals are not Hindus but the latter ignored the idea, even though it came from a distinguished academic authority.[25] In this regard, V. F. Vineeth once stated:

> In spite of the dominant Sanskrit culture, the truth remains that many millions of Northern Indians are tribals and Adivasis and Dalits who are, strictly speaking, not Hindus; they are counted as Hindus for the sake of the privileges of the high class but are mercilessly neglected and marginalised as far as their own identity and welfare situations are concerned.[26]

S. M. Michael holds the view that the biggest agent of conversion in Indian history has been Brahminic Hindus. According to him, the powerful upper castes of a particular area exercised such an influence on the lower castes and outcastes that they also wanted to be integrated into the caste hierarchy by adopting the values and practices of the upper castes. This process is described as "sanskritization" by the

---

[25] Cf. *ibid.*, 364. As mentioned by T. K. Oommen during a lecture at Vidya Jyoti, Delhi Srinivas did not even acknowledge the letter that was sent in this regard (*ibid.*).

[26] V. F. Vineeth, "Theological Formation in the North Indian Context of Religious Pluralism," in *Third Millennium* 12, 4 (2009) 30-31.

well known anthropologist M.N. Srinivas.[27] The dominant society in India would like tribals to fall in line with the sanskritization process. Here Brahmins are the determining factor in life. Sanskritization is considered as a way out in order to gain *mukti* (salvation) and there is a question where to place the tribals in the caste-ridden social structure of Indian society.[28] In this situation Hindus naturally wish to put the tribals in the Hindu flock with low caste title. This process of Hinduvisation of tribals is going on with full political party support by the Governments[29] especially ruled by the parties of Hindu organisations.

> The highest number of conversions was effected through the Hindu Census enumerators. The question in the census usually is: What is your dharma? Dharma is a word generally alien to tribals, particularly where formal education has not reached. Consequently, all adivasis (tribals), except those who are baptized into Christianity or Islam, are simply categorized as Hindu.[30]

---

[27] Cf. M. N. Srinivas, *The Cohesive role of Sanskritization and Other Essays*, Oxford University Press, Delhi 1989, p. 56; S. M. Michael, "Real Issues Behind the Violence," 16. "Once a tribe came under the influence of the Brahminical people and was converted into a caste enjoying monopoly in a particular occupation, a strong tendency was set up within it to remodel its culture more and more closely in conformity with Brahminical way of life" (N. K. Bose, *Culture and Society in India*, Asian Publishing House, Bombay, 1967, 214).

[28] Cf. N. Minj, "Meaning of Tribal Consciousness," in *Religion and Society*, 36, 2 (1989), 22.

[29] Cf. A. Patel, "Hinduisation of Adivasis: A Case Study from South Gujarat," in *Dalits in Modern India: Vision and Values*, S. M. Michael (ed.), Vistaar Publications, New Delhi 1998, 189; S. M. Michael, "Real Issues Behind the Violence,"16.

[30] S. M. Michael, "Real Issues Behind the Violence," 16.

It should be pointed out that the distaste of Hindus generally in relation to conversions seems to operate in favour of the Arya Samaj and other Hindu groups associated with them in *Suddhi*. While many Christians were taking a liberal view and insisting on conversion as spiritual experience, the Arya Samaj has continued its proselytising to win back converts to the Hindu fold. One independent member strongly opposed the introduction of the Bill, but Mr. Aggarwal of the Jana Sangh strongly endorsed the Bill, which was eventually passed into law. Similarly, in Madhya Pradesh, legislation had been enacted to prohibit conversions— and similarly in the state of Orissa. In three states, the ideology of *suddhi* has succeeded in closing the door to the loss of power through conversion to other religions.[31]

"Inhabitants of India in the beginning were not Hindu. Hinduism is the religion of Aryans and not of India's original inhabitants who have their own gods, goddesses, spirits, forms of worship, rites, rituals, theology, etc. A great debate on proselytizing Indian tribals goes on, and missionaries are constantly under attack that they are destroying the religion and cultures of Indian ethnic communities, making them part of other religions. But the vast majority of the tribals or indigenous populations of India, much more than the Christian missionaries, are being converted to Hinduism making them Dalits within the *varna jati* systems."[32]

The Arya Samaj and the VHP promote this kind of reconversion process not only in India, but all over the

---

[31] Cf. J. F. Seunarine, *Reconversion to Hinduism through Suddhi*, 81-82.

[32] This is an idea expressed by Mahipal Bhuria, a well-known anthropologist, who also belongs to a tribal group, in an interview with the author.

world.[33] This process is catching fire among the tribals in North India. The tangible evidence is seen at present in Orissa after the violent attacks and the demand put forward towards the tribals who wish to come back to their village. Conversion from Christianity to Hinduism is catching fire in North India and is called *ghar vapsi* or 'homecoming'; it is stated in an article by S. M. Micheal in the following words:

> Conversion from Christianity to Hinduism is encouraged and supported by the Sangh Parivar as *Ghar Vapsi* or homecoming.[34]

After the recent acts of violence against Christians in Orissa a very brutal form of re-conversion process organised by Hindu fundamentalists was witnessed. Christians wanting to return to their homes were told by Hindu extremists to "come back as Hindu or don't come back at all." Many who dared to return to their villages were forcibly converted to Hinduism. Sometimes Hindu extremists poured petrol over the Christians and asked them to convert; if they refused, they were burnt. Many Christians were burned and, in some cases, cut into pieces because of their refusal to be converted into Hinduism.[35]

ॐ

---

[33] Cf. S. M. Michael, "Real Issues Behind the Violence," 19.
[34] S. M. Michael, "Real Issues Behind the Violence," 15.
[35] Cf. S. Vecchia, "Orissa, il drama di mogli e madri," 1,5.

CHAPTER 2

Challenges from the Accusation of Detribalisation

The initial years embracing Christianity involved a break with the past. Dancing, use of drums, consumption of alcoholic drinks, old myths and sacrifices were frowned upon as being devilish. Missionaries did not understand the importance of certain tribal rules with regard to eating, marriage within the tribe, etc., with the result that in certain cases Christian converts lost their tribal status and were looked down upon as a caste apart.[1] No doubt the Christian tribals got early benefit of modern education and were more progressive in outlook in accepting the modern

---

[1] Cf. A. Tirkey, "The Tribal Churches in India: It's Identity and Challenges Today," in *Jeevadhara*, 33 (2003), 322. Jesus was an inculturated man of his time and of his society. In his action the Church has the model of what she herself should do. Christ points out to her the path she must follow in order to make her mission more effective and fruitful (J. MANATHODATH, *Culture, Dialogue and the Church: A Study on the Inculturation of the Local Churches According to the Teaching of Pope Paul VI*, 48). The author has taken following words of Pope Paul VI as the basis of his affirmation: "The path of direct contact, psychological affinity, and an identity of life-style with the peoples to whom the Gospel is to be announced" (PAUL VI, "Message for Mission Sunday," 21 October 1973, in *Teachings* VI, 1973, 299).

western values. But alienation from tribal culture and its way of life at times created the rift between the Christian tribals and the non-Christian tribals within the same community, where the economic allurement was the cause of accepting Christianity.[2] One of the accusations against Christian missionaries on detribalisation is as follows:

> Christian missionaries entered the tribal area as social reformers but their other motive had been to convert the tribals to Christianity. The result was that tribals who embraced Christianity, left their own culture and started adopting the others (western) culture.[3]

Detribalisation in Religious Practices

Fear of losing one's tribal identity still looms large in the minds of ordinary people. There are certain agencies and groups that aggravate the fear-complex in the minds of people. It is, therefore, very important that we properly analyse and understand the implications of a change of tribal religion. It goes without saying that there are biases, rumours and prejudices associated with conversion of tribals to Christianity. Although Christianity has not been controversial in western countries, it raises the eyebrows of many in Asian countries, and more particularly in India because of its association with colonial rule. The same amount of blind hatred and bitterness is showered on Christianity as on other traces of colonialism.[4]

There is a general perception amongst the dominant Hindu castes that the Christian mission has destroyed tribal culture and heritage, which in turn, has had an adverse effect on their identity. They say that as tribal people accept Christianity,

---

[2] Cf. H. C. Upreti, *Indian Tribes: Then and Now*, 153.

[3] *Ibid.*, 207.

[4] Cf. C. Lakara, "Christianity and Tribal Identity," in *Religion and Society*, 34, 2 (1989), 33.

they abandon their traditional religion and culture and have thus become "detribalized." Every now and then there has been a call to stop the activities of the Christian mission amongst the tribals.[5]

In all humility and truthfulness, one has to admit that embracing Christianity has not been an unmixed blessing. It has brought about a split in the community between those who profess the traditional religion and those who have embraced Christianity, and amongst the latter a further splitting into various denominations. The weakening effect on tribal society, as expressed, for instance, in the erosion of authority of the original *panchayat*, is a loss we Christians do not sufficiently appreciate.[6]

> It is true that Christianity has brought division in Tribal society. Christian tribals no longer participate in the tribal religious rituals or in many cultural activities expressed in music, song, dance and drama. There is also division between the traditional tribals who stand for strict adherence to customs and cultures, and the Christian tribals who, in the light of the new awakening and western values, have become more liberal in their outlook and interpretation of life.[7]

---

[5] Cf. D. L. Touthang, "Tribal Identity and Contemporary Christian Mission in India," in *Drishtikone*, 3 (1995), 5.

[6] Cf. A. Tirkey, "The Tribal Churches in India: Its identity and Challenges Today," in *Jeevadhara*, 33 (2003), 322.

[7] D. L. Touthang, "Tribal Identity and Contemporary Christian Mission in India," 5. This same view is also expressed by another tribal scholar: "Christianity has brought division in tribal society, because the Christian Tribals no longer participate in the Tribal religious rituals. They have stopped celebrating Tribal festivals and many customs of the traditional society have been abandoned. This however, differs from one Christian denomination to another" (C. Lakara, "Christianity and Tribal Identity," 33-34).

In the common man's estimation, Christianity is adversely affecting tribal identity. With the acceptance of the Christian religion, tribals are abandoning their traditional religion (animism, nature worship, etc.), and as a result, going out of the tribal society. This was the point taken in the Lok Sabha by the late Minister of State Mr. Martik Oraon in the mid-sixties. This has concrete reference to the suit against the late Mr. David Munjini taken to court by Kartik Oraon when the dispute over the candidature from the Lohardaga reserved constituency had arisen. The verdict was given in favour of Mr. Munjini, confirming that change of religion does not change his tribal origin and identity. Time and again, the call against Christian conversion has been given mostly by politicians and others with vested interests.[8]

Christians have been accused–and rightly so–of contributing to the detribalisation of society. Formal education has for a long time neglected the teaching of tribal languages and literature. The same education has promoted middle class values, which equip persons and families to cope with modern life and formal employment, but have brought along an erosion of traditional tribal values.[9]

Detribalisation in Lifestyle Affecting Tribal Unity and Solidarity

Alienation from the traditional society also indirectly affected tribal unity and solidarity. Christianity brought education, which further brought an awareness of better social life, improved health and sanitation, etc. There was a clear distinction between a Christian tribal and a non-Christian tribal, at least in the beginning. The sense of superiority was

---

[8] Cf. C. Lakara, "Christianity and Tribal Identity," 32-33.

[9] Cf. A. Tirkey, "The Tribal Churches in India: Its Identity and Challenges Today," 322.

deeply instilled in the minds of tribals. The non-converted were looked down upon as illiterate and backward.[10]

The educated tribals are proud of western education and values imbibed in mission schools, but they are also aware of the danger of succumbing to fashionable trends in dress and dances of the film world. Invasion of modernity, the "Coca-Cola" generation, television and cinema are making the tribal cultural elements reel and lose their anchor. Young boys and girls, in their quest for higher education, are caught up in the process of detribalisation. We cannot stop these trends. The question before the tribals now seems to be how and whether they can make a happy blend of their tribalness and what the brave new world keeps on offering them.[11]

Economic and educational deprivations were responsible for an ever widening gap between the two groups. Christians were quick to take to primary and higher education. Economic progress was natural with the increase of education. But it was also seen that some of the highly educated westernised Christians looked down upon their own tribal brethren as backward and uncivilised, as drunkards and criminals. The bias in favour of conversion deprived other tribals of the benefits of the missionary educational institutions. They believed that missionary educational institutions were meant to convert people to Christianity. Many abstained from attending missionary institutions, while other non-tribals thronged these institutions and benefited the most out of such educational opportunities.[12]

---

[10] Cf. C. Lakara, "Christianity and Tribal Identity," 34.

[11] Cf. P. Tete, "Christian Missions and Tribal Identity," in *Sevartham*, 24 (1999), 59.

[12] Cf. C. Lakara, "Christianity and Tribal Identity," 34.

Detribalisation in Art and Language

Throughout India a deep sense of art, and of aesthetics generally, can be seen being expressed, exhibited and retained in various forms in indigenous people. They are in the forms of costumes, bead ornaments, weaving, tattoos, wood carving, language, dance, music, festivals, paintings like Pithoras, wall paintings, bamboo works, metal art, mimicries, etc., which even though not sufficiently promoted are being retained and giving human or ethnic identity. If retained they will also give psychological affirmation to their culture and personality. Tribal languages, which are an inherent part of their life, bring great joy in communication, which is not replaced when they are acculturated. It should be retained since it is the folklore of the common people.[13]

Language is a medium of expression. It is a people's particular code, a field where collective identity and the perception of reality are constantly reformulated; therefore, one cannot get into self unless one knows it. One cannot delve deep into the tribal culture unless one speaks the language. These days quite a number of educated tribal youths, particularly the urban ones, do not speak their mother tongue. Even if they speak it they stuff it with Hindi or English words out of ignorance or snobbery or mere laziness.[14] Many of them had their complete school and higher education residing in hostels run by the Christian missionaries.

During the British rule Indian Christianity spread its roots in the tribal habitation and the 'missionaries' who were entrusted with the task of reform in tribal areas, opened educational institutions. In these schools, at times, the medium

---

[13] Cf. M. Bhuria, *Adivasikaran: Tribalisation and Aboriginalisation,* 12.

[14] Cf. P. Tete, "Christian Missions and Tribal Identity," 59.

of instruction was English. Missionaries started giving education to Christian tribals through the Roman script. The result was that these people forgot their own dialect/language. There was also the accusation that the motive behind this introduction of the English language and the Roman script is to spread Christianity.[15]

Christian service has undone something and done many things to enrich tribal consciousness. 'Missionisation' in the ordinary sense of the term does more damage than good to tribals. The missionary contribution to tribal language and literature is praiseworthy; missionary motivation for the weak and marginalised is quite necessary for the tribals to care for each other.[16] We also have to consider the valuable contribution of Christian missionaries to Bhil literature through various books and the famous grammar book in the Bhil language by a European missionary.[17]

---

[15] Cf. H. C. Upreti, *Indian Tribes: Then and Now*, 153, 207.

[16] Cf. N. Minj, "Meaning of Tribal Consciousness," 23.

[17] L. Jungblut has published a grammar book in Bhili language which is appreciated by many (cf. W. KOPPERS - L. JUNGBLUT, *Bowmen of Mid-India*, Acta Ethnologica et Linguistica, Wien 1976, vol. 1, 251).

CHAPTER 3
Challenges from the Incongruity of Missionaries

Besides the external challenges, there are also challenges pertaining to the incongruity emerging from missionaries' relation with local culture and authentic religious life according to one's faith. These are the defects seen in the missionaries' personal life and community life. It is easy to blame the external problems that become obstacles in evangelisation. But rarely does one notice the internal deficiencies within oneself and one's own community. Therefore, in this section, we are dealing with defects of the missionaries which are to be overcome for better evangelisation among the tribals in North India. Hindsight can show that there are many such defects challenging evangelisation. We have taken three such dimensions for our consideration: inefficiency of deep-rootedness in local culture and one's own faith, defects in the formation and inefficiency of incarnated and solidarity-forwarded movement on the part of missionaries.

Insufficiency of Deep-rootedness in Local Culture and in One's Own Faith

Projection of foreign Church keeps a distance from the local people and becomes an obstacle in the smooth running of evangelisation and getting success in efforts.[1] India, after having western colonialism and the coming of missionaries with the colonisers, has already gained a stigma from the Indians. Again missionaries continue to project an image of the Western Church that strengthens the opportunities for more accusations and for keeping a distance. This lack of deep-rootedness can be seen in various spheres: construction of Churches and institutions, lifestyle of missionaries, language, etc. This situation can pour oil on the flames when fundamentalist Hindu organisations are propagating a "one culture one nation" attitude. We have already seen that there is a move to put the tribals into the Hindu fold and here, in this section, it is good to mention the words of Gowalkar, one of the ideologues of RSS:

> The non-Hindu people in Hindustan must either adopt the Hindu culture and language, must learn to respect and revere Hindu religion, must entertain no idea but to the glorification of the Hindu nation, i.e. they must not only give up their attitude of intolerance and ingratitude towards this land and its age-long traditions, but must also cultivate positive attitude of love and devotion instead; in one word they must cease to be foreigners or may stay in the country wholly subordinated to the Hindu nation claiming nothing, deserving no privileges, far less, any preferential treatment, not even citizen's rights.[2]

---

[1] "In Asia there is a fairly widespread opinion that the Church is something foreign and Western. Normally in the analysis of the problem, the cause is attributed to the fact that the Christian faith was imported from Europe and presented under the European guise and also that work of evangelisation was linked to European colonialism. Sometimes the Church is considered guilty of having kept out of the normal life of the people, of their history, their struggles and their aspirations" (J. Dinh Duc Dao, "Evangelisation and culture in Asia: problems and prospects," 76).

[2] M. S. Golwalker, *We or Our Nationhood Defined*, Bharat Prakashan, Nagpur 1938, 52, as cited by T. N. Madan, *Modern*

In the opinion of Chacko Valiaveetil, the very fact that we speak about inculturation implies that our faith and life are not fully inserted into Indian culture, or in other words, that our Christian and religious life remains something foreign to India. We may not like to admit this. Yet, the people who look at us from outside, our Hindu friends, frankly tell us this without meaning any offence. We belong to the Indian soil and everything Indian has a connaturality with us. If our life is to blossom forth and produce rich fruits in abundance, it must draw sustenance from the native soil.[3] At present, Christianity in India is visualised as the following symbolic statement:

> Christianity in India may be said to be still in its pot of western trappings. Only when she is freed from these trappings and allowed to strike roots into the rich soil of Indian wisdom and holiness it can bear fruits in abundance.[4]

Myths, Locked Minds: Secularism and Fundamentalism in India, Oxford University Press, New Delhi 2003, 223; F. MINJ, "The Politics of Conversion: A Theological Reflection on the Current Debate on Conversion in Tribal India," in *Sevarthan*, 30 (2005), 153.

[3] Cf. C. Valiaveetil, "Inculturation: The Need and the Scope," in *Indian Missiological Review*, 9, 1 (1987), 24-25. "Religious and spiritual sense deeply rooted in the culture should establish an interior disposition that fosters acceptance of the Gospel; instead, in several cases, it seems that it is the deeply religious nature of the culture that has been a great obstacle for the presentation of the Gospel. So we need to understand more fully the significance of religion in the Asian cultures" (J. DINH DUC DAO, "Evangelisation and Culture in Asia: Problems and Prospects," 72).

[4] C. Valiaveetil, "Inculturation: The Need and the Scope," in *Indian Missiological Review*, 9, 1 (1987), 25.

At this juncture, it is also important to make a reflection on the phenomenon of the westernisation of Christians and the westernisation of people of other faiths. One may say that many Hindus are more westernised than the Catholics. Unfortunately, this movement embraced the whole world in which the Christians in general and the Catholics in particular are only a part of it. But this cannot be a valid reason to avoid inculturation in Mission if one is aware of the incarnational approach of Jesus Christ. We have to concentrate more on the aspect of Jesus' approach than the cultural aspect. A missionary has to go for inculturation because it was the approach of Jesus in his mission. This way of reflection towards inculturation may remove the confusion with regard to more emphasis on to the culture than the Gospel. The approach of Jesus in mission is the only way that can be fruitful in executing one's mission.

To be rooted in the local culture and strong in the faith is an urgent need of the time. When the Church wants to take the side of the people it often finds itself going against the Government. And the Church is in many cases hesitant to offend the government. This is because Churches are rootless. They have not gone deep into the soil of this country and they are very shallow in their Christian understanding. Therefore, they feel very shaky in dealing with the Government. The dependency on money makes it still harder for the Church to take the side of the poor. They make statements, but when it really comes to taking the side of the poor it becomes very difficult because the Government will pounce.[5]

Authentic witnessing of Gospel is required in contemporary evangelisation. Christian missionaries should

---

[5] Cf. N. Minj, "Forum," in *Drishtikone*, 3 (1995) 12.

be so deeply rooted in Indian culture and history that they have enough courage to face even the Government. Secondly, missionaries have still not gone deep into our Christian teachings and way of life. They have inherited something and they repeat that rather than creatively going into it themselves in such a way that it becomes a part of their life.[6] Once Gandhiji expressed the significance of authentic witnessing of Gospel values from the part of Christian missionaries in a challenging tone to the question of Stanley Jones: "How can we make Christianity naturalized in India?" Gandhiji answered:

> First, I would suggest that all of you Christians, missionaries and all, must begin to live more like Jesus Christ. Second, practice your religion without adulterating it or toning it down. Third, emphasize love and make it one's working force, for love is central to Christianity.[7]

Defects in the Formation

Defects in the formation of missionaries would also reflect in the life of future missionaries and in the result of their missionary activities. Therefore, sufficient care should be given in the level of formation of future missionaries according to the area where they are supposed to be in service. In the words of V. F. Vineeth:

> Theological training is not simply training in the vacuum. It is training in the actual living context to answer the living challenges of our time. Today in India, especially in North-India, the religious challenge is not simply of pluralism, but of a militant Hinduism, a religion which has become an ideology, a political consciousness which wants to make itself by all means felt. This phenomenon

---

[6] Cf. *ibid.*, 13.

[7] Qutoed in Stanley Jones, *Mahatma Gandhi: An Interpretation*, Lucknow Publishing House, Lucknow 2000, 65.

forces us to wake up and have a critical look at our religion and theological formation.[8]

An authentic inculturation comes from an inculturated Christology. There has been a serious and systematic attempt to develop a tribal Christology by the regional theologates and the tribal theologians yet a satisfactory result is still to come. The lack of a tribal Christology affects the very life, mission and evangelisation of the Church. Perhaps this lack of Christology leads the "Sangh Pariwar" to brand the tribal Christians as "foreigners" even in our own land.[9]

A proper study of tribal religion is necessary for the missionaries who intend to be among the tribals. The first challenge is to understand tribal religions. Earlier missionaries also misunderstood this, unfortunately, and that has been a setback. The third and fourth generations of Christians and Churches have to understand the positive aspects of tribal culture. There are many wrong understandings of tribal religion, derogatory remarks, etc. Even some of our own people have developed that attitude, which is completely wrong. Therefore, the first challenge is that the Christian Churches in tribal areas must involve themselves a little deeper in relating to tribal religion.[10]

With the increasing influence and impact of materialism, secularism, and liberalism in the post-colonial era, tribal people continue to experience challenges and stagnation in spirituality. These include loss of focus in discipleship and

---

[8] V. F. Vineeth, "Theological Formation in the North Indian Context of Religious Pluralism," 41.

[9] Cf. F. Minj, "The Politics of Conversion," 155; J. TIRKEY, "Tribal Values and the Principle and Foundation," in *Sevartham*, 32 (2007), 37.

[10] Cf. N. Minj, "Forum," 13.

spiritual formation, loss of indigenous wisdom, character and values and infiltration of western culture and ideology through the neo-Pentecostal and new religious movements. Information technology and military power contribute to the decline of indigenous cultures and discrimination against minorities.[11]

> The perception that the present classical and western pattern of theology with that of dogmatic nature does not address the existential issues and problems of *adivasi* society, prompted its introduction into the curriculum. Seen from the present-day context of *Adivasi* society – which is undergoing various forms of sufferings – the present trend of western theology seems to be quite irrelevant.[12]

Many in India look to the aspect of poverty in the life of a religious person with great respect and reverence, as a person who has renounced the world in order to seek God. Ordinary people go to them for guidance and to find ways and means to approach God through them. In a way, Christians, especially the religious, play a greater role in their witness to Christ, in the poverty of their life.[13] The future missionaries among the tribals require, above all, to witness with quality of life and therefore they should be formed well during the formation period to become persons who from their very life project as spiritual persons. Comforts and comparatively high facilities in the formation houses really become a defect in

---

[11] W. Longchar, "Tribal Theology in the Changing Context," 94-95.

[12] A. S. Hemron, "Towards a Programme of Contextual and Adivasi Theology," in *Religion and Society*, 50, 3 (Bangalore 2005), 87.

[13] Cf. T. A. Swamy, "The Spirit of Poverty, an Essential Witness in Priestly Life in Indian Context," in *Indian Theological Studies*, 40, 3 (2003), 273.

forming efficient missionaries among the poor tribals, who in general, live with basic minimum material comforts and commodities of life.

In the present situation, it is not simply religious pluralism that challenges the evangelisation in North India, but an emerging power of religious fundamentalism. "To answer this challenge, first of all we should strip ourselves off all traits of religious fundamentalism and develop a non-aggressive pattern of life. At the same time, our theological training must be deeply religious, very authentic, very profound."[14] A challenging situation created by the defective formation system of missionaries is also a matter of consideration in the present time. This situation is clear in the thought-provoking words of A. Poruthur:

> We seem to place great importance on academic training almost neglecting personal formation. Providing intellectual answers by stacking courses upon courses and clearing one examination after another is a lop-sided method to initiate a person into the realm of spirituality. The number of priests quitting in recent times has not opened our eyes still to deduce a simple conclusion that there is something missing in the long drawn-out process.[15]

Insufficiency of Incarnated and Solidarity-Forwarded Movement

The solidarity-forwarded movement through an incarnational approach is another challenge faced by missionaries. The Church has to identify with the tribal communities in their struggles. Without that solidarity-forwarded movement

---

[14] V. F. Vineeth, "Theological Formation in the North Indian Context of Religious Pluralism," 42.

[15] A. Poruthur, "Ground Realities of North Indian Mission", in *Mission Today*, 6 (Shillong 2004), 158.

evangelisation among the tribal communities will be slow.[16] Missionaries have to be one with the tribal community in their sorrows and struggles through an incarnational approach. The indigenous people find difficulty in relating with the missionaries due to the lacking of belongingness. A sense of belongingness, through coming down to the discomforts of indigenous people, experiencing their sorrows, is becoming a challenge for evangelisation among the indigenous people. In other words, Jesus' kenotic approach is necessary on the part of missionaries. The effectiveness of evangelisation also depends on constant contact with people:

> The touchstone of pastoral effectiveness is the constant contact with the people. This is something deeper than and beyond the presence or absence of structures and institutions. One can live in a slum or a village and yet be extremely selfish; one can live in an elaborate parish complex and be marvellously approachable. But all things being equal, obviously, the former style does open up many more homes and hearts.[17]

Missionaries to some extent failed to show in action their responses towards the agony of Christ, which is extended in the sufferings of the tribals. This challenge hits at the very roots of our Christian existence and calls for conversion at the very level where we are supposed to live the mystery of

---

[16] Cf. N. Minj, "Forum," 13.

[17] H. Hendriks, "Pastoral Pioneering Among Tribals," in *Third Millennium*, 1, 4 (1998), 69. The realisation of some religions in relation with the comforts they enjoy in comparison with the poor whom they serve is mentioned by Francis J. Moloney: "We are not really poor. We have plenty to eat, cars to move about in, a roof over our heads and a warm bed every night. Most of all we do not experience that terrible insecurity about 'tomorrow' that the truly poor experience" (F. J. Moloney, *Disciples and Prophets: A Biblical Model for the Religious Life*, Crossroad, New York 1981, 85-86).

Christ. The agony and passion and resurrection and glorification of Christ are various aspects and phases of the one Christian mystery, and the evangeliser has to live and lead his people from their agony and despair to re-creation and glorification, from the old world of misery, suffering and sub-human life to the state of fully developed human beings and sons and daughters of God in the new earth and new heaven where God will wipe away their tears and make them sing a new canticle of Moses in joy and peace.[18] Indifference of missionaries to the burning issues in the life-struggle of tribals and remaining closed for their own security creates a distance between tribals and missionaries.

> "I have come in order that they may have life—life in all its fullness" (Jn. 10:10). This was the mission of Jesus that God's kingdom may come and his will be done on earth... We must "give flesh" to these statements in terms of what it means to bring that fullness of life to actual people in specific and concrete situations. With the sort of life do they struggle for, and how it is found, received and shared? The answer can never be discovered in the abstract. We must be there first. We cannot say what it means until we go to people, stay with them, listen and learn what it means to talk about that life which Jesus wants for them.[19]

There are the social, economic and political challenges facing the tribals. These issues have to be understood by the Churches and then responded to in a creative way.[20] The problems of

---

[18] Cf. D. S. Amalorpavadas, *The Theology of Indirect Evangelisation,* NBCLC, Bangalore 1969, 20. "If you, Christians really believe," said Ashok Mehta, "that the agony of Christ is extended in the sufferings of the masses, you must show it in action" (*ibid.*).

[19] J. A. Scherer - S. B. Bevans (eds.), *New Directions in Mission and Evangelisation – 1: Basic statements 1974-1991,* Orbis Books, Mary Knoll, N Y 1992, 57-58.

[20] Cf. N. Minj, "Forum," 13.

poverty, injustice and exploitation also have become journey partners in the lives of tribals. These problems are not the dangers but the challenges of life. Growing poverty and unemployment have forced them to take unlawful activities. "They are not able to enjoy the fruits of development in its true sense of productivity due to the injustice and exploitation by the people of upper stratum."[21] Education can play a great role in increasing the economy of these tribals and enabling them to occupy a good place in the community. These problems are the challenges for the Bhil literate tribals, who are well settled in life. A solution to these problems is possible only if they are constantly made aware of the value of education, government policies and developmental programmes. Missionaries have to take it as a challenge and be actively involved in these burning issues.

Solidarity with the poor becomes more credible if Christians themselves live simply, following the example of Jesus. Simplicity of life, deep faith and unfeigned love for all, especially the poor and the outcast, are luminous signs of the Gospel in action. The Synod Fathers called on Asian Catholics to adopt a lifestyle consonant with the teachings of the Gospel, so that they may better serve the Church's mission and so that the Church herself may become a Church of the poor and for the poor.[22] For example, the practice of walking between the villages considered to be a good case where effectiveness may not be equated with just efficiency alone. Walking takes more time, but we do meet a lot more people, and stay longer in their houses, and also have more time for

---

[21] Sahu, *Tribal Culture and Identity*, Sarup & Son, New Delhi 1998, 216.

[22] Cf. John Paul II, Post-Synodal Apostolic Exhortation *Ecclesia in Asia* (6 November 1999), 34.

thinking and praying.[23] With all modern facilities, to a certain extent, missionaries keep away from the poor local people. Missionaries are able to get the fastest transportation available, but this not only keeps them at a distance from the local people they serve, but also affects intimate contact. If one believes in quantity, then these kind of modern means will serve but not for the quality of service. Thus, the "solidarity" approach has a strong dimension of qualitative success in evangelisation through inculturation:

> Only when the Christian message of salvation in Jesus Christ takes the saving need of the poor seriously, becomes human with them in solidarity, can the process of 'inculturation' succeed. It will be the result of the cultural consciousness of a Christian community which strives with the poor to overcome their poverty.[24]

---

[23] Cf. H. Hendriks, "Pastoral Pioneering Among Tribals," 67.

[24] J. G. Piepke, "Incarnation in Cultural Context," in *Indian Missiological Review*, 12, 1(1990) 49.

CHAPTER 4

Priorities in Missionary Formation

The Conciliar decree *Ad Gentes* recommends deepening the missionary formation for the apostles who dedicate themselves to evangelisation with various dimensions, spiritual and moral, doctrinal and pastoral formation.[1] This formation is to be carried out in seminaries, novitiates, apostolic groups or movements and, especially, in missionary institutes, in order to ensure not only perseverance in spiritual life, but also permanent and effective apostolic action. This initial formation should be completed and continually reaffirmed all through life—a suitable ongoing formation.[2]

The missionary's fidelity, spirituality and generous perseverance depend to a great extent on the formation received in the initial period and during the subsequent periods of apostolic life.[3] Formation of missionaries according to the area of service is a very important element in relation with

---

[1] Cf. AG 25, 26.

[2] Cf. J. Esquerda Bifet, "Missionary Spirituality", in *Mission for the Third Millennium*, Pontifical Mission Organization, Bangalore 1993, 349.

[3] Cf. J. Esquerda Bifet, *Spirituality for a Missionary Church*, Urbaniana University Press, Roma 1994, 111.

the success of mission. Besides common formation, each person has to receive an orientation in accordance with the local culture and ethos of the place of evangelisation. This missionary formation also needs an updating and re-orientation in view of the contemporary changes in the society where one is being sent to proclaim the Gospel. Many of the above-mentioned challenges can be confronted better through sound formation in tune with those challenges. "Missionaries must always meditate on the response demanded by the gift they have received, and continually keep their doctrinal and apostolic formation up to date."[4]

Reorientation of Missionaries

Incarnating the Gospel in people's cultures is a need of the time. Missionaries who come from other cultures and countries must immerse themselves in the cultural milieu of those to whom they are sent. So they must learn the language of the place in which they work, become familiar with the important expressions of the local culture and discover their values through their direct experience.[5] Promotion of tribal culture is one of the aspects to be considered with great

---

[4] John Paul II, Encyclical Letter *Redemptoris Missio* (8 December 1990), 65.

[5] Cf. RM 53. "There is a need to present Christ and His message in a way that is suited to indigenous ethos and genius. This entails giving importance to the narrative and, in a sense, downplaying the purely theoretical and primarily doctrinal. Though *Ecclesia in Asia* seems to be specially preoccupied with the Asia of the great world religions and, therefore, does not make pointed reference to the indigenous peoples and their cultures we can still draw inspiration from the directives therein: to consider the task of bearing witness to Jesus Christ as the supreme service that the Church can offer to the people of Asia" (D. Jala, "What the Church can do with/for Indigenous Peoples," 49-50; cf. EA 20).

importance during evangelisation among tribals. Thus, missionaries can project the image that missionary activities do not damage traditional and valuable tribal culture; rather, due respect and tribal identity are maintained. A lot of importance needs to be given to incarnate the Word of God in the tribal culture.

There should be re-orientation for the missionaries towards the evangelisation of culture and creating an atmosphere for Jesus to be born in the local culture. Therefore, it is rightly observed by J. Manathodath that the process of evangelisation of cultures is not a process of destruction. The Church does not demand that everything that does not conform in all details to the Gospel should die. She only insists that whatever is sinful be eliminated. As to the "seeds of the Word" that exist in cultures, she recognises them, carefully preserves them and contributes to their growth. The teaching of Jesus Christ and his redemption have to be considered as the complement, renewal and bringing to perfection of all that is good in human tradition. In other words, he himself tried to promote whatever was good in existing cultures.[6]

In the opinion of G. Plathottam, missionaries have to adopt a lifestyle that is more attuned to the larger ethos of the country, especially the tribals, and greater emotional integration. These concerns, far from being academic issues, must be studied dispassionately and with openness to the Spirit.[7] This affirmation can be understood in its right sense only when one is able to read it at the level of the incarnational

---

[6] J. Manathodath, *Culture, Dialogue and the Church: A Study on the Inculturation of the Local Churches According to the Teaching of Pope Paul VI*, 48-49.

[7] Cf. G. Plathottam, "Religious Fundamentalism, Media Blitzkrieg and Our Response," in *Mission Today*, 2 (2000), 37.

approach of Jesus for the salvation of humanity; Jesus' birth and life in the concrete cultural ethos of a country.[8] Otherwise it may give an opening to a debate as to which is important: "the ethos of the country" or "the Gospel." A deeper understanding of the distinction between the Gospel and the culture into which it was born for the first time in history is necessary in order to have a correct vision of the mission of Christ. Otherwise one may try to pluck out the Gospel, which is born or has grown up in the ethos of a particular country or culture, and transplant it in another country. This idea may be expressed in a moderate way, such as missionaries being invited to model their life after the Gospel, keeping the ethos in the culture of the people to whom they bring the Gospel. The need for the re-orientation of the missionaries is also felt in the FABC meetings and is reflected in one of its preparation papers:

> Church personnel, especially bishops, priests, sisters and seminarians, should be exposed to theology in Indigenous/ Tribal context. Seminaries that cater to Indigenous/Tribal areas have a special obligation to develop and teach theology in such an Indigenous/Tribal context.[9]

---

[8] "The Word of God was made flesh. He became incarnate in a particular society, in a particular place and time. He assumed the human nature from inside and thereby mode of existence which he did not have previously. He spoke the language of his country and drew on local life for the examples with which to illustrate his teachings of justice, truth, hope and love" (J. Manathodath, Culture, Dialogue and the Church: A Study on the Inculturation of the Local Churches According to the Teaching of Pope Paul VI, Intercultrual Publications, New Delhi 1990, 47. Cf. PAUL VI, "Homily during Mass at Stadium, Djakarta," 3 December 1970, in *AAS* 63, 1971, 77).

[9] S. Karotemprel, "The Indigenous/Tribal Peoples and a Renewed Church in Asia," in FABC Papers – No. 92g, Thailand 1995, 13.

Ongoing formation was an initiative of Vatican II mainly for priests and similarly for all workers for evangelisation "especially in view of the circumstances of modern society."[10] It requires constant adjustment and capacities. This is applicable for the missionaries who are committed to evangelise the indigenous people. In the present situation, spiritual strengthening is more needed and it is worth remembering the teachings of the Church in relation with the ongoing formation of priests: "An opportunity of increasing their knowledge of pastoral methods and theological science, and at the same time strengthening their spiritual life and sharing the pastoral experiences with their brother priests."[11]

Promotion of Local Vocations and Lay Missionaries

In the level of people's acceptance, the local missionaries have more opportunity than the outsiders. This is due to the acquaintance with the local language and culture, and moreover, belongingness in the heart of the people. Therefore local tribals either with a special vocation as full-time evangelisers or as the lay apostolate will have more possibility of success than missionary evangelisers. Encouragement has to be given to the tribals to come out for evangelisation. Therefore, the Church proclaims "an attitude of deep respect for their traditional religion and its values; this implies the need to help them to help themselves, so that they can work to improve their situation and become the evangelisers of their own culture and society."[12]

---

[10] *Optatam Totius*, Decree on the Priestly Formation, (28 October 1965), 22.

[11] *Presbyterorum Ordinis*, Decree on the Ministry and Life of Priests (7 December 1965), 19.

[12] EA 34.

The FABC also recognises this view of efficiency of tribals in evangelising their own people in comparison to the missionaries from outside for the same service. It is indigenous or tribal Christians themselves who can best evangelise their own people, but the encounter between the Gospel and indigenous or tribal peoples does not end at baptism. True inculturation occurs when a people, under the guidance of the Holy Spirit, bring together the Gospel teaching with their own cultural values.[13]

The world of Asian indigenous people, varied as it is, is rich in promise and continues to challenge Christian evangelisers to commit themselves anew to the immense task of living and witnessing to the Gospel in the context of indigenous cultures.[14] Pope John Paul II expressed this witnessing role of lay faithful in an Apostolic exhortation: "Witnessing to the Gospel in every area of life in society, the lay faithful can play a unique role in rooting out injustice and oppression, and for this too they must be adequately formed."[15]

To the laity belongs the task of bringing the witness of the Gospel, its meanings and values, into every area of the temporal order and of thus working to renew the structures of the economic, social and political life of Indian society and

---

[13] Cf. Fabc, "Message of the FABC consultation on "Indigenous /Tribal Peoples in Asia and the Challenges of the Future," (Pattaya, Thailand, 18 December 2001) in *Indigenous Peoples in Asia and Challenges of the Future*, M. D. Saturnino (ed.), Claretian Publications, Bangalore 2004, 187-188.

[14] Cf. Fabc, "Recommendations of the Conference," in *Evangelisation among the Indigenous Peoples of Asia: A Report of a Conference on the Concerns of Indigenous Peoples Hua Hin, Thailand, September 3-8, 1995*, FABC Papers, no. 80, 43.

[15] EA 45.

of all human relationships within it: this is their task; their baptism and confirmation lays it upon them; they may show it, and Indian Catholics are called to respond to it with an initiative, courage and responsibility worthy of their vocation. Their Christian commitment also demands that they participate in the work of evangelisation. Catechists are of invaluable service to the Church, great attention should be paid to providing them with suitable training.[16] In this regard, Pope John Paul II exhorted:

> Within missionary activity, the different forms of the lay apostolate should be held in esteem, with respect for their nature and aims. Lay missionary associations, international Christian volunteer organizations, ecclesial movements, groups and solidarities of different kinds - all these should be involved in the mission *ad gentes* as co-operators with the local Churches."[17]

The egalitarian nature of tribal society has to be recognised and adopted in the system of the Church in the sphere of evangelisation. The tribals are used to taking decisions after consultation with the village, clan or tribe. Even though the Church is essentially a hierarchical and sacerdotal community, in all matters that do not belong to sacred orders, there could be a rethinking. Laity and youth, in particular, have played, and still play, a crucial role in direct evangelising work and catechesis, particularly by means of "home catechesis," through preaching at the so-called "prayer meetings." They also make an important contribution to the planning and organisation of expressions of popular religiosity, such as religious processions and parish administration.[18]

------

[16] Cf. D. S. Amalorpavadas, *Theology of Evangelisation: in the Indian Context*, NBCLC, Bangalore 1971, 41.

[17] RM 72.

[18] Cf. S. Karotemprel, "The Indigenous /Tribal Peoples and a Renewed Church in Asia," 13.

> Clerics and religions should adapt themselves to the Indigenous/Tribal ethos of egalitarianism in all matters that do not pertain to sacred orders and the exercise of sacred authority. They should let the laity in their Churches exercise the roles they are traditionally known to perform.[19]

The success of evangelisation among the indigenous peoples owes much to the role played by lay people, who often had to undergo severe trials in order to bear witness to the faith and bring others to Christ.[20] John Paul II in *Ecclesia in Asia* appreciated the significant role of the lay faithful in evangelisation. "To them I express the thanks of the whole Church, and I encourage all lay people to assume their proper role in the life and mission of the People of God, as witnesses to Christ wherever they may find themselves."[21]

Contextual and Tribal Theology in Formation Houses

One of the pertinent issues that have to be considered among the challenges for evangelisation among the tribals in North India is the training of the clergy and Church leaders within the socio-cultural and political milieu of the country and a deeper commitment to promote contextual theology.[22] As it was recommended by the Apostolic Exhortation Ecclesia in Asia:

---

[19] S. Karotemprel, "The Indigenous /Tribal Peoples and a Renewed Church in Asia," 13.

[20] Cf. FABC, Recommendations of the Conference on Evangelisation among the Indigenous Peoples of Asia, Hua Hin, Thailand, September 3-8, 1995, in FABC Papers- No. 92g, Thailand 1995, 16.

[21] EA 45.

[22] Cf. G. Plathottam, "Religious Fundamentalism, Media Blitzkrieg and Our Response," 37.

In the past, formation often followed the style, methods and programmes imported from the West, and while appreciating the service rendered by that mode of formation, the Synod Fathers recognized as a positive development the efforts made in recent times to adapt the formation of evangelisers to the cultural contexts of Asia. As well as a solid grounding in biblical and patristic studies, seminarians should acquire a detailed and firm grasp of the Church's theological and philosophical patrimony.[23]

Theology needs to be done in an indigenous/tribal context rather than in the western context. It will give greater prominence to narrative theology and oral traditions. In order to do such theologising, we need to develop an indigenous/tribal theological language. [24] Integration of tribal theology in theological education, especially in North India, where many are preparing to be missionaries among the tribals, may enable the future missionaries to become competent ministers of teaching, caring and liberating the poor and leading the people to a fuller humanity.[25] It is at this juncture that there

---

[23] EA 22.

[24] Cf. S. Karotemprel, "The Indigenous /Tribal Peoples and a Renewed Church in Asia," 13.

[25] Cf. W. Longchar, "Tribal Theology and Theological Education in India," in *National Council of Churches Review*, 121 (Nagpur 2001), 580. Tribal theology is defined as: "The tribal theology, both as concept and practice, emerged towards the end of eighties in response to different forms of barbaric atrocities, human rights violation, ethnic conflict, poverty, injustice, ecological destruction and Hindu philosophical tradition of Indian Christian theology. It is an attempt to express Christian faith in socio-cultural, traditional and liturgical and thought patterns of the people. The experience of oppression and hardship, stories, myth, symbols dances, songs, and the tribal people's spirituality become vital source for doing theology" (*ibid.* 582). Definition according to A. S. Hemron: "It is doing

comes the need to have a re-orientation in our theological outlook and exercises, and here comes our programme of contextual theology. We tend to train our students primarily with this contextual theological orientation; so that once they go back to the masses with this new mindset, they may address the societal needs of the people side by side with their usual Church ministry. Their societal involvement, which they do as part of their 'theological activism' may thus help bring in the betterment of the hitherto ailing *adivasi* society that constitutes the *adivasi* Church[26] Tribal theology has two dimensions: liberation and inculturation. Theology in the tribal context of India needs to touch both these aspects, as tribals are, in general, subjugated by others and have their own significant cultural context that cannot be neglected.

In other words, the primary task of contextual theology is to help people understand the text in relation to their particular context. Such a theological reflection helps people to translate the Gospel message to the needs and aspirations of the people in question. Therefore, like other contextual theologies, tribal theology is also contextual, a theology from 'below' and from the underside of history. It seeks to reflect

---

theology from the Adivasi (Christian Adivasi) perspective. It seeks to re-read and re-interpret the gospel from Adivasi-Christian perspective so as to make the gospel message relevant to the Adivasi life-situation now marked/ characterized with varieties of socio-political and human problems. In this process it comes under the category of contextual theology. As contextual theology, it seeks to relate the gospel message as "God-given-answer to human problems." In its spirit and orientation, it is therefore an 'answering theology' (A. S. HEMRON, "Towards a Programme of Contextual and Adivasi Theology", in *Religion and Society*, 50, 3 [2005], 88).

[26] Cf. A. S. Hemron, "Towards a Programme of Contextual and Adivasi Theology," 87-88.

on the faith experience of the tribal people and aims to liberate tribals from their inferiority complex, from oppression and discrimination, by attempting to rediscover the liberating motifs from the tribal culture and reinterpreting the Bible and Christian traditions. So, the focus and goal of tribal theology is liberation. It embraces social, economic, cultural, political and ecological dimensions. In the process of working for their own liberation, tribals work for the liberation of both the oppressor and the exploited. It is, therefore, a theology which includes the liberation of all humanity and of God's creation.[27]

The second dimension of tribal theology is a theology of inculturation. Culture and tradition are what determine the uniqueness of tribal people and unite them as a community. Culture is an authentic source for a theology of inculturation. When the Gospel is integrated into the social and cultural life of the people, it becomes a meaningful sign to them and to others as well.[28]

A theology of inculturation among the tribals in India has the following implications:

- An acceptance and conviction that the tribal cultures are good and beautiful. They are never inferior to non-tribal cultures

- A realisation that the Gospel and culture are never contradictory but that culture forms the substratum for the Gospel and the latter is the soul of culture

- A willingness to accept and integrate all the positive elements of tribal cultures into Christian theology and belief system

---

[27] Cf. W. Longchar, "Tribal Theology and Theological Education in India," 582.

[28] Cf. J. Saldana, *Inculturation*, St. Pauls Publications, Mumbai 1997. 54; B. L. Mawrie, "Experience of the Tribal Socio Political, Historical and Cultural Context: Quest for a Tribal Theology," in *Mission Today*, 7 (2005) 55.

- A deliberate effort to preserve and promote the rich cultural heritage of tribal communities.[29]

Theologians, especially from India, consider that the development of a tribal Christian theology is inevitable. The meeting of the Christian faith with these tribal religions is open to the Light, Truth and Goodness found in them.[30] The pressing need for giving a missionary perspective to theological studies was repeated on various occasions after Vatican II by the Congregation for Catholic Education. Speaking of the study of theology, the Dicastery observes:

> It is called to interpret, support and serve the growing operative impulse of the Church's new missionary awareness. This occurs above in the relations with non-Christian religions and cultures, with which it is necessary to establish an encounter and hold a dialogue, which will draw spirits close to each other and make a new form of evangelisation possible.[31]

---

[29] Cf. B. L. Mawrie, "Experience of the Tribal Socio Political, Historical and Cultural Context: Quest for a Tribal Theology," 56.

[30] Cf. A. Parapullil, "Tribal Theology," in *Sevartham*, 2 (1977), 28.

[31] Congregation for Catholic Education, La formazione teologica del futuro sacerdotale (The Theological formation of the future Priest), Rome, 1976, n. 27, 12-13. Cited in J. Saraiva Martns, "The Missionary Formation of Priests in the Light of the 1990 Synod and the *Pastores Dabo Vobis*," in *Mission for the Third Millennium*, Pontifical Mission Organization, Bangalore 1993, 349.

CHAPTER 5

Priorities in Witnessing
Gospel Values

People today put more trust in witnesses than in teachers, in experiences than in teaching and in life and action than in theories. The witness of a Christian life is the first and irreplaceable form of mission. Jesus Christ, whose mission we continue, is the witness *par excellence* and model of all Christian witnesses. The Holy Spirit accompanies the Church along her way and associates her faith with the witness he gives to Christ.[1] Evangelisation is not mere theoretical teaching about Christ, an apologetical argument about Christianity, but a sharing of the Christian experience– a testimony to the transforming interpersonal relationship brought about between man and God and among men by and in Jesus Christ. To tell another what one has seen, heard, touched and experienced is called bearing witness. This is what Christ asked of those men who had experienced him (cf. Mk. 16:15). 'You will be my witnesses not only in Jerusalem, but throughout Judea and Samaria, and indeed to the ends of the earth' (Acts.1:8).[2] "Modern man listens more willingly to

---

[1] Cf. EN 41; RM 42.

[2] Cf. D. S. Amalorpavadas, *Theology of Evangelisation: in the Indian Context*, 22-23.

witnesses than to teachers, and if he does listen to teachers, it is because they are witnesses."[3]

Life Witness of Missionaries

The first form of witness is the very life of the missionary, of the Christian family and ecclesial community, which reveals a new way of living. The missionary, in spite of his or her human limitations and defects, should live a simple life taking Christ as the model.[4] Thus, the way of presenting the Gospel is as important as the life of the person who presents it.[5] This is certainly true in the Indian context, where people are more persuaded by holiness of life than by intellectual argument. "The witness of life has become more than ever an essential condition for real effectiveness in preaching. Precisely because of this we are, to a certain extent, responsible for the progress of the Gospel that we proclaim."[6] This effectiveness of life witness in proclaiming the Gospel of Christ was expressed by Mahatma Gandhi as his expectation from Christian missionaries in India:

> Let your lives speak to us, even as the rose needs no speech but simply spreads its perfume. Even the blind who do not see the rose perceive its fragrance. That is the secret of the Gospel of the rose. But the gospel that Jesus preached is more subtle and fragrant than the Gospel of the Rose.[7]

---

[3] Paul VI, Address to the Members of the *consilium de laicis* (2 October 1974): *AAS* 66 (1974), 568; EN 4.

[4] Cf. RM 42.

[5] Cf. J. Dinh Duh Dao, "Evangelisation and Culture in Asia: Problems and Prospects," 75.

[6] EN 76.

[7] M. K. Gandhi, *Harijan*, 17, 4, 1937, quoted in J. Thazhathukunnel, "Mahatma Gandhi's Attitude to Mission," in *Ishvani Documentation and Mission Digest*, 21, 2 (2003) 204.

A friendly approach on the part of missionaries can win the heart of people. This approach of missionaries to indigenous people should be different from that of other people, especially the usual exploiters. In the past, the missionaries' approach among the tribals in India has been recognised and appreciated very much by the tribals themselves.[8]

A genuine evangelisation among Indian tribals consists in the realisation that there can be no true proclamation of the Gospel unless missionaries offer the witness of lives in harmony with the message they preach. Missionaries will be credible in their relations with the people and in proclamation of the message, only if this love is manifested in living simply, following the example of the poor Jesus. Like Jesus the model, a missionary spirituality finds its expression in a witness of life that speaks the Gospel so eloquently that it is heard not only by the ears of the body, but also by the ears of the heart, that it is seen not only on the printed page, but in the life witness of the messenger.[9] In this regard, Mother Teresa once expressed: "There should be less talk; a preaching point is not a meeting point. What do you do then? Take a broom and clean someone's house. That says enough."[10]

---

[8] A testimony from a tribal bishop: "And how could the missionaries who were bearers of this Gospel come all the way without knowing us. You see all through our history we have never found a friend, and missionaries were the first people who came as friends. This really clicked. Other people exploited us, but these were friends who wanted to help us. They had no intention of exploiting us, but throughout history people had come just to exploit us" (N. MINJ, "Forum," 13).

[9] Cf. EA 34; cf. B. A. Maheu, "A Missionary Spirituality for Asia Reflections on Ecclesia in Asia," in *Mission Today*, 2, 3 (2000), 320-321.

[10] Mother Teresa, *A Gift for God: Prayers and Meditations*, compiled by Muggeridge M., Harper & Row, New York 1975, 45.

The people of India also appreciate doers than preachers, and this can be understood from the words of the most respected person in India, Mahatma Gandhi, the father of nation. Once Mahatma Gandhi expressed his view about people who led a life with witnessing value; "Their lives are silent, yet most effective testimonies. . . . I can say that a life of service and uttermost simplicity is the best preaching."[11] This attribute of the Indian mind was rightly understood by John Paul II who recommended life witness of missionaries in the proclamation of Good News in Asia:

> This proclamation is a mission needing holy men and women who will make the Saviour known and loved through their lives. A fire can only be lit by something that is itself on fire. So, too, successful proclamation in Asia of the Good News of salvation can only take place if bishops, clergy, those in the consecrated life and the laity, are themselves on fire with the love of Christ and burning with zeal to make him known more widely, loved more deeply and followed more closely.[12]

An exemplary life of holiness is expected on the part of missionaries for successful evangelisation, as it was expressed by Paul VI in his Apostolic Exhortation: "The world calls for and expects from us simplicity of life, the spirit of prayer, charity towards all, especially towards the lowly and the poor, obedience and humility, detachment and self-sacrifice. Without this mark of holiness, our word will have difficulty in touching the heart of modern man."[13] A missionary who has no deep experience of God in prayer and contemplation will have little spiritual influence or missionary success. This is in

---

[11] M. K. Gandhi, *Harijan*, 29, 3, 1935, quoted in J. Thazhathukunnel, "Mahatma Gandhi's Attitude to Mission," 204.
[12] EA 23.
[13] EN 76.

particular true of the situation in Asia, where other non-Christian spiritual traditions follow so much of prayer and contemplation. Therefore, the future mission in India depends to a great extent on contemplation.[14] This same idea is more developed in *Ecclesia in Asia*:

> A genuinely religious person readily wins respect and a following in Asia. Prayer, fasting and various forms of asceticism are held in high regard. Renunciation, detachment, humility, simplicity and silence are considered great values by the followers of all religions.... Christians who speak of Christ must embody in their lives the message that they proclaim.[15]

Prophetic Witness and Work for Liberation

Alienation and marginalisation is a problem faced by the Indian tribals where the Church can intervene with its prophetic voice in becoming the voice of the voiceless. The Church can be a powerful agent of conscientisation of the tribals in their given area. The Church can provide legal aid to support the cause of indigenous peoples. It can unite scattered indigenous populations for more effective and collective actions against the process of alienation.[16] The Church has to support the cause of tribals who seek a just and equitable recognition of their identity and their rights, especially helping them to get a just solution to the complex

---

[14] Cf. RM 91.

[15] EA 23. "La Chiesa non ha bisogno solo di più missionary, ma missionary di profondo spiritualità: audaci e fervorosi nell'impegno, e innamorati di Cristo e del suo Evangelo, tanto da volere farLo concocere a tutto il mondo e condividere con la gente l'esperienza di Lui" (J. Dinh Duc Dao, "La spiritualità Missionaria", in *Cristo Chiesa Missione*, Pontificia Universitas Urbaniana, Roma 1992, 386).

[16] Cf. S. Karotemprel, "The Indigenous/Tribal Peoples and a Renewed Church in Asia," in FABC Papers–No. 92g, Thailand 1995, 9-10.

quest of the alienation of their lands. This alienation is a common problem for the tribals in India and the seriousness of this situation can be understood in this statement: "Between 1951 and 1990 at least 18.5 million people have been displaced by development projects. This totals up to more than 2 percent of the India population and around 27 percent of the tribal population in India."[17]

The Church in Asia cannot ignore this plight (disharmony and disappearance of traditional social functions due to industrialisation) of the indigenous people. Its action for the development of the people has to be two-pronged: it must see to the integral growth of the people, while ensuring that sustainability is not jeopardised. The key word here is "empowerment" of the people. No true development work, which makes people perpetually dependent, can be supported.[18] In this regard, John Paul II invited our attention through his encyclical, which states:

> The Church is called to bear witness to Christ by taking courageous and prophetic stands in the face of the corruption of political or economic power; by not seeking her own glory and material wealth; by using her resources to serve the poorest of the poor and by imitating Christ's own simplicity of life. The Church and her missionaries must also bear the witness of humility, above all with regard to themselves – a humility which allows them to make a personal and communal examination of

---

[17] W. Fernandes, "Indian Tribals and the Search for an Indigenous Identity," in Social Change, xxiii, 2&3, 1993, 37, quoted in M. G. Kariapuram, "Government Policy Towards the Tribals and Tribal Alienation in India," Indian Missiological Review, vol. 19, 3, (1996) 30.

[18] Cf. D. Jala, "What the Church can do with/for Indigenous Peoples," 46.

conscience in order to correct in their behaviour whatever is contrary to the Gospel and disfigures the face of Christ.[19]

The Indian Church can conscientise tribals about their rights and duties according to the Constitution and Laws of India. The Church can give moral support to the political struggle to obtain legal and economic benefits, privileges and rights.[20] There are various governmental commissions for the welfare and protection of the tribals in India. The prime task of the missionaries in this aspect would be enabling the tribals to know about the various welfare projects in their favour and at times being with them to get their rights.

The tribals of India are faced with the challenge of economic exploitation and discrimination. The Church can join other voluntary organisations in supporting the rights of tribals, keeping in mind the ultimate benefits of all concerned. The Church can help to illumine and form the moral and social conscience of governments, financiers and industrialists to rise above exclusively capitalistic considerations. The human person must be the point of departure and arrival of all economic, industrial and political planning and considerations.[21]

An evangeliser, as a person dedicated to the service of God and humans, has to be deeply concerned about forces of disintegration that are destroying the religious and moral values by which our people have lived for centuries.[22] The list

---

[19] RM 43.

[20] Cf. S. Karotemprel, "The Indigenous/Tribal Peoples and a Renewed Church in Asia," 10.

[21] Cf. *ibid.*, 11.

[22] Cf. D. Bhatt, "Evangelisation in the Context of Hindu Culture and Religion of North India," in *Mission Today*, 7 (2005), 345.

of evils is illustrative and not exhaustive of the distressful moral situation of North India. What is more disheartening is that some of these evils have the sanction of society. Religious and other social structures are built to perpetuate them. North India groans for liberation from all these evils, which have rocked the very foundations of society. They are looking for a messiah. Amidst what looks like an alarming picture, we also see signs of hope.[23] Bishop N. Minj recalled the valuable contribution of the Church in giving justice to the tribals in the past:

> The Church tried to seek Justice for the people in the last Century. They tried fighting for the people's lands. The missionaries and mission societies, not all but some, really fought for the land for the people. And the kind of exploitations and injustices which were rampant were in some way alleviated because the Church or the Gospel came in and people became conscious of themselves and stood up for their own rights.[24]

The existence of fundamentalism and fanaticism in India today demands from missionaries a heroic witnessing, like that of the prophets. Their life is also like that of the prophet, a living message for others. "The martyr, then, is not only a hero and a witness who is ready to bear witness if necessary even unto death, but he is also one who dies in order to bear witness, a person whose death itself is a testimony of the God of the Christian faith."[25] According to N. Minj, a few individuals and groups are trying to opt for the poor tribals and are trying their best to work for justice and against the exploitative

---

[23] Cf. *ibid.*, 346.

[24] N. Minj, "Forum," 12.

[25] A. Cabezon, "Martyrdom: The Supreme Mark of Greatness," in *Philippiniana Sacra*, 15, 44 (1980), 228.

systems at work amongst these tribal people. But when the entire system seems to be so vicious, the contribution of the Church is minimal.[26]

Promotion of Christian Values through Witnessing of Charity

The importance of witnessing through Christian charity is highlighted by John Paul II in his encyclical: "The evangelical witness which the world finds most appealing is that of concern for people, and of charity toward the poor, the weak and those who suffer."[27] Jesus lived out what he preached to others. He emptied himself by living among the people, sharing in their hopes and sufferings and giving his life on the Cross for all humanity. This kenosis enables the missionary to leave his place, to accept the new land, and its people, to accept their culture and to be a light to them.[28] This way of witnessing charity leads to an increasing awareness of human rights, sources of social problems, social justice and the responsibility of creating a situation in which people enjoy the privileges granted by God.[29]

There is a need for Christ-like action in the genuine service of poor tribals, coming down to the level of the poor and

---

[26] Cf. N. Minj, "Forum," 12.

[27] RM 42.

[28] Cf. C. Kochupurackal, *India Awaiting the Good News*, G. M. Secretariate, Cochin 1988, p. 35. "We must go to the poor, but go to them with a heart filled with God and familiar with the Gospel in order to give them God and his Gospel, helping them to discover God and his Gospel, helping them to discover God and live the Gospel precisely in their situation as poor people" (J. Dinh Duc Dao, "Present-day situations of the mission *"ad gentes"*: at the service of the poor," in *Omnis Terra* 27 [Eng. ed., 1993] 293).

[29] Cf. M. T Paulose, "Evangelisation in India Today," in *Sevartham*, 23 (Ranchi 1998), 118.

knowing them well through the experience of their suffering, opening the heart to love the poor and becoming living witnesses of God's mercy.[30] Jesus had compassion for sufferers: he felt for the blind, the sick, the maimed, the hungry, the homeless, the captive and the lonely. He came to heal them, spoke to them in endearing terms, brought them hope and told them that they counted before God. Yes, they are important, for God who created them out of love keeps loving them. [31]

A majority of tribals in India still live in poverty, suffering economic hardship and exploitation. Therefore, there is the challenge for contemporary Christian mission amongst the tribals to be concerned with economic issues and justice.[32] In the midst of various economic problems faced by the tribals, there is a need of a helping hand from others to resolve and liberate the tribals from their pathetic living conditions. As long as they are living in the present backward situation the powerful ones will go on subjugating them in various ways. Here lies the scope of charitable witnessing of missionaries and enlightening them with Christ's love.

Charity and the mission of preaching go hand in hand. Jesus was always concerned about the physical needs of his listeners and had compassion for the multitude that followed after him. Sometimes he even missed his meals; he forgot to eat.[33] Jesus left us a beautiful example from his life and taught

---

[30] Cf. Mother Teresa, *No Greater Love*, B. Benenate - J. Durepos (eds.), New World Library, Novato 1997, 102.

[31] Cf. E. Le Joly, *Mother Teresa: Messenger of God's Love*, St. Paul's Publications, Bombay 1988, 116-117.

[32] Cf. D. L. Touthang, "Tribal Identity and Contemporary Christian Mission in India," 6.

[33] Cf. Mother Teresa, *No Greater Love*, B. Benenate - J. Durepos (ed.), 99.

us how charity and missionary preaching are connected to each other. This aspect is reflected well by Blessed Mother Teresa and expressed through the following words:

> How did he (Jesus) put his compassion into practice? He multiplied the loaves of bread and the fish to satisfy their hunger. He gave them food to eat until they couldn't eat any more, and twelve basketfuls were left over. Then he taught them. Only then did he tell them the good news. This is what we must often do in our work: we must first satisfy the needs of the body, so we can then bring Christ to the poor.[34]

Much is written about preaching in voluntary poverty. This can be done very congenially when we actually share people's lives and homes. It also has the twin benefit of making our gospel-message more transparent and credible. There is also a special joy, and sometimes a struggle (and not always a successful one), to try to make Christ's "sell all" "no place to lay his head" more real. Living with the poor tribals in their village was a very natural way to try to do this.[35] This is called serving the poorest of the poor and "imitating Christ's own simplicity of life."[36] This implies that Christians ought to speak through their lives, by their total understanding and acceptance, sharing and helping one another in the concrete situation in which they live. "This witness should provoke questions in the non-Christians' mind – why do Christians live in such a manner? Who inspires them? This is an essential element of evangelisation, which silently proclaims the good news."[37]

---

[34] Mother Teresa, *One Heart Full of Love*, J. L. González – Balado (ed.), Servant Publications, Ann Arbour, Michagan 1984, 2.

[35] Cf. H. Hendriks, "Pastoral Pioneering Among Tribals," 67.

[36] RM 43.

[37] C. Colaco, *25 Years "Ad Gentes" in India*, Asian Trading Corporation, Bangalore 1991, 58; M. T. Paulose, "Evangelisation in India Today," in *Sevartham*, 23 (1998), 118-119.

Charitable services, especially educational charity, play an important and supportive role in the evangelistic work going on amongst the tribals. The literacy programme not only helps the people to become aware of their rights, but also helps people in reading the Bible and understanding its teachings. In this way, people's faith is consolidated. The education that we provide for children will enable them to be effective leaders of the Church in the future. The credit assistance programme, which is built on group accountability, brings a sense of responsibility among the community and teaches them to be faithful. The health and other welfare programmes that are implemented reflect God's mercy upon the people.[38]

All charitable services function as an entry point for the Christian workers to share God's love with the tribals. There are many examples of this taking place in India. Working to free the tribals from the exploitation and injustice that they face on a daily basis is important as we seek to reflect God's character. Indigenous people see this and many respond.

Also, special care has to be taken while involving the charitable services that it has to be the outcome of Jesus' vision and able to impart the message of Christ. Contrary to this would be a charity remaining only in the social dimension and missionaries may drift away from the ultimate purpose of their vocation and mission to a particular group of people commissioned by Jesus. The mission of Church is always necessary but must not be seen only related to material and social problems. According to J. Dinh Duc Dao:

---

[38] Cf. K. Dhanabalan, "Serving Tribal People," in *Drishtikone,* 3 (1995), 9.

We must go to the poor, but go to them with a heart filled
with God and familiar with the Gospel in order to give
them God and his Gospel, helping them to discover God
and live the Gospel, precisely in their situation as poor
people.[39]

---

[39] J. Dinh Duc Dao, "Present-day situations of the mission "ad
gentes": at the service of the poor," in *Omnis Terra*, Eng. ed.,
February (1993) 293.

CHAPTER 6

Priorities in Inter-Religious and Cultural Aspects

Religion and culture play a very important role in the communitarian life of tribal society. Religious rites and rituals are central in the life of a tribal community. The social life of a tribal society has a strong religious background that holds the community together and gives it a distinct identity. Culture gives tribal people a framework of meaning, which is preserved in language, thought patterns, ways of life, attitudes and symbols and is celebrated in art, song, music, dance, drama, and life. If religion is the key to unity and cohesion in tribal society, culture is the collective memory and heritage handed down from generation to generation, which helps to maintain a distinct identity and character.[1] As far as the Asian local Churches are concerned, theologising until very recently was dependent on western models and categories of expression. Some effort has been made to theologise using models and categories of the dominant cultures of Asia, such as Hinduism and Buddhism. It is also urgent to begin to theologise in the context of indigenous/

---

[1] Cf. D. L. Touthang, "Tribal Identity and Contemporary Christian Mission in India," 5.

tribal cultures.[2] The principle of interreligious dialogue, "Mutual enrichment through adoption of whatever is positive and valuable in each other's religion,"[3] has to be the concern while setting up relations with traditional religion of Indian tribals.

Healthy Relation with Local Religions and Inculturation

In the midst of various threats from fundamentalism and religious fanatics, a missionary has to give priority to having a healthy relationship with existing local religious leaders and leaders of fundamentalist religious organisations. This relationship has to develop at the very beginning of entrance to an area of service. Many a time one realises its need when some atrocities occur in his or her life. If this has developed earlier, to a certain extent, atrocities can be avoided or can get certain support from the leaders of those religious groups. Inter-religious dialogue and inculturation may be some of the means of having healthy relations with the members of other religions: "The penetrating insight into peoples and their cultures, exemplified in such men as Giovanni da Montecorvino, Matteo Ricci and Roberto de Nobili, to mention only a few, needs to be emulated at the present time."[4] As regards strengthening the relations with other religions further, let us take a look at the Encyclical:

> Interreligious relations are best developed in a context of openness to other believers, a willingness to listen and the desire to respect and understand others in their

---

[2] Cf. S. Karotemprel, "The Indigenous/Tribal Peoples and a Renewed Church in Asia," 13.

[3] B.Kanakappally, "Dialogue and Proclamation with Hinduism," in *Correspondence Course on Missionary Formation*, Ponitfical Missionary Union – International Secretariat, Rome 1997, 15.

[4] EA 20.

differences. For all this, love of others is indispensable. This should result in collaboration, harmony and mutual enrichment.[5]

God, by assuming human culture, has sanctified all cultures. Jesus was a deeply historical and human reality sharing in our flesh, man among men, like us in all things though never closing himself to God through sin. Nothing that is truly human was foreign to Jesus. He lived a life of full involvement, earning his daily bread by his labour as a carpenter. He spoke Aramaic, the language of the common people, and when he wanted to explain his doctrines he used examples in abundance from the daily life of the people. For the institution of the Eucharist he picked up bread and wine from the dining table. As one Indian theologian puts it in the context of inculturation, had Jesus used, instead of the bread and wine from the table, some exotic beverage imported from elsewhere, or had he used Latin or Sanskrit instead of Aramaic for his thanksgiving for the breaking of the bread, he would not have been loyal to his mission.[6] Paul Tillich perceptively remarks:

> "The form of religion is culture. This is especially obvious in the language used by religion. Every language, including that of the Bible, is the result of innumerable acts of cultural creativity... There is no sacred language

---

[5] *Ibid.*, 31. "I repeat how important it is to revitalize prayer and contemplation in the process of dialogue. Men and women in the consecrated life can contribute very significantly to interreligious dialogue by witnessing to the vitality of the great Christian traditions of asceticism and mysticism" (*ibid.*). Cf. John Paul II, Post-Synodal Apostolic Exhortation *Vita Consecrata* (25 March, 1996), 8: *AAS* 88 (1996), 383.

[6] Cf. C. Valiaveetil, "Inculturation:The Need and Scope," 26-27.

> which has fallen from a supernatural heaven and been put between the covers of a book...”[7]

Inculturation literally means insertion into culture. By culture what is meant is the general lifestyle of a people that is expressed through their customs, dress, food-habits, literature, music, art, architecture, folklore, worship, festivals, etc. In our context, therefore, we may define inculturation as the process by which our Christian faith and life are inserted into the culture of India.

The Church can accomplish her mission only in a way that corresponds to the way in which God acted in Jesus Christ: he became man, shared our human life and spoke in a human language to communicate his saving message. The dialogue that the Church proposes is grounded in the logic of the Incarnation. Therefore, nothing but fervent and unselfish solidarity prompts the Church's dialogue with the men and women of Asia who seek the truth in love.[8]

There is an intimate bond between evangelisation and inculturation, as has been clearly pointed out in the Church's magisterium.[9] People encounter the Gospel within their culture. Culture, which is dynamic, shapes and is shaped by humans. It is the obligatory path for an evangeliser to present the faith in a way that takes the cultural richness of the peoples into consideration. In doing this, the cultures too are refined and renewed.[10] Therefore, Pope John Paul exhorted: "This

---

[7] P. Tillich, *Theology of Culture*, Oxford University Press, 1959, 47, quoted in Vicente G. Cajilig, *Dialogue between Faith and Culture: Towards Integral Human and Social Development*, Lucky, Manila 1998, 48.

[8] Cf. EA 29.

[9] Cf. *ibid.*, 21.

[10] Cf. D. Jala, "What the Church can do with/for Indigenous Peoples," 50.

engagement with cultures has always been part of the Church's pilgrimage through history. But it has a special urgency today in the multi-ethnic, multi-religious and multi-cultural situation of Asia, where Christianity is still too often seen as foreign."[11]

Through inculturation the Church makes the Gospel incarnate in different cultures and at the same time introduces peoples, together with their cultures, into her own community. She transmits to them her own values, at the same time taking the good elements that already exist in them and renewing them from within.[12] Through inculturation, the Church, for her part, becomes a more intelligible sign of what she is and a more effective instrument of mission.[13] At the same time, the Church also has to avoid the possible danger of syncretism in the life of Christian tribals and it is significant to recall the statement of J. Dinh Duc Dao:

> Since elements of religiosity are rooted in their culture, which are the basis of their individual and common identity and personality, if they are not harmonized with the new outlook of the Gospel, their personality will remain divided and consequently their life will be disjointed. With these persons, dialogue leads necessarily and dynamically to inculturation.[14]

The present inculturation efforts of the Church are to a certain extent on a peripheral level. The aim of inculturation is not to gather tribals into a clerical Church, but to 're-birth' the Church among tribals. We must not be satisfied with a banana Church or a coconut Church–yellow/brown (Asian) on the

---

[11] EA 21.

[12] Cf. EN 20; RM 52.

[13] Cf. RM 52.

[14] J. Dinh Duc Dao, "Proclamation and Dialogue with the Traditional Religions of Asia and Oceania," 5.

outside yet remaining white (foreign) on the inside. We work towards a mango Church–yellow (Asian) through and through.[15] This idea was reflected in one of the papers presented at a FABC conference with regard to traditional religions:

> True inculturation goes beyond the adoption of external practices, symbols and language. It is grafting on to whatever is true and notable. Traditional religions are expressions of the bountiful treasures which God has bestowed on peoples. The Gospel is to be grafted on to the living tree of traditional religions. The Church would be poorer without their religious wisdom. It can enrich the Christian for it shares in the unfathomable wisdom of God.[16]

---

[15] Cf. J. M. Prior, "Faith and Culture in Dialogue: A Reflective Theological Synthesis," in *Word and Worship*, 39, 5 (2006), 325. "The Second phase of inculturation is a profounder experience of our very apostolate; and it synthesizes several aspects of all we have said earlier. Daily we bump into so many fellow human beings: shopkeepers, rickshaw-pullers, farmers, anyone – Punjabis Dalits, Bengalis, Marwaris, Tribals, etc. As soon as our relationship deepens, they normally share with us what they really seek, and hope, fear, and hate, and love, and enjoy . . . somehow Christ, as he is incarnate here and now, embodies and answers all those quests, and hopes, and fears, and loves. . . . As someone has said, the difficulty with inculturation and evangelisation is not opposition from other groups, but perhaps our own inability for such a self-emptying. The true pastor is indeed called to be another Christ!" (H. Hendriks, "Pastoral Pioneering Among Tribals," 71).

[16] S. Karotemprel, "Traditional Religions," in FABC, "Recommendations of the Conference," in *Evangelisation among the Indigenous Peoples of Asia: A Report of a Conference on the Concerns of Indigenous Peoples Hua Hin, Thailand, September 3-8, 1995*, FABC Papers: no. 80, 28-29.

Promotion of Tribal Culture through Tribalisation Movements

The best way to preserve what is good in a culture is to evangelise that culture. If we want to preserve the riches of indigenous or tribal cultures, we must strive to bring the Gospel to those peoples who have not yet been blessed by the Good News of Jesus Christ.[17] The Church transforms cultures, but also accepts what is positive in them. This is borne out by the history of the Church, but is of greater urgency today in Asia where Christianity is still too often seen as foreign.[18]

The process of 'Hinduisation' has been taking place all through the known history of India. The *adivasis* or tribals have been absorbed into the superimposition of their superiority over other racial people of India. Jayant Lele explains this process: "The Brahminic worldview had succeeded on several occasions in the past in capturing the diversity of cults, deities, sects and ideas (by making many compromises) under the rubric of *Sanatana dharma*."[19]

In the midst of the claim that indigenous people are part of Hindus and the re-conversion process led by fundamentalist Hindu organisations, the new approach introduced by M. Bhuria, *advasikaran* (tribalisation), is appropriate. The accusation against Christians about detribalisation will also be answered well if Christian missionaries can work for tribalisation – a process in which tribals can regain their traditional cultural values and life. Thus tribalisation can be

---

[17] Cf. FABC, "Message of the FABC Consultation on "Indigenous /Tribal Peoples in Asia and the Challenges of the Future", (Patty, Thailand, 18 December 2001) in *Indigenous Peoples in Asia and Challenges of the Future*, M. D. Saturnino (ed.), 187.

[18] Cf. *ibid.*, EA 21.

[19] J. Lele, *Hindutva: The Emergence of the Right*, Earthworm Books, Madras 1995, 13.

a neutral solution in a period of forced conversion to Hindu religion by fanatical and militant Hindu organisations.

> *Adivasikaran* (Tribalisation) is a significant and permanent process for a peaceful restoration; re-introduction of native cultures, re-affirmation and re-organising of every native good elements of tribes of the world is the main basis. This way we envisage a clear-cut plan for restoring peacefully past heritage of native societies in the world. Besides this, innovate, and integrate every good thing from any culture of natives and of the world, especially in relation to education, technology, languages, media, etc.[20]

Hindutva snatched away the original inhabitancy of tribals. The *Hindutva* ideologies have worked out a clear strategy to establish the Aryans as the original inhabitants of India. They started replacing the word *adivasi* with *vanvasi*. The original inhabitants of India (*adi-vasi*) are now turned into simply people of the jungles (*van-vasi*). This is yet another attempt to retain the Aryan hegemony over the gullible tribal people. Most of the Catholics belonging to this ethnic category are blissfully ignorant of the carpet pulled from under their feet. Hardly any organised protest is carried out even in regions where there is sizeable Catholic absence.[21]

Precisely, when the Church is being accused, in places, of being responsible for the cultural alienation of the indigenous people, we need to show the true picture of how it is the Church that, through the process of inculturation, actually promotes the cultural richness of tribals. This is all the more urgent when indigenous peoples tend to face crises.[22] In the

---

[20] M. Bhuria, *Adivasikaran: Tribalisation and Aborignalisation*, 7.

[21] Cf. A. Poruthur, "Contemporary Challenges for Mission in North India," 364.

[22] Cf. D. Jala, "What the Church can do with/for Indigenous Peoples," 51.

opinion of M. Bhuria, *adivasikaran* (tribalisation) is a sacred and viable concept and a noble mission towards forging a cultural path of tribal and native people's total innovative development in the world today. Each tribe and indigenous aboriginals have inherited an age-old significant and noble heritage, which they lost in the course of time due to various adverse circumstances.[23] One needs to go deeper to its cultural roots and revive the native traditions honestly.

The immediate challenge for Indian tribals at the moment is to save their tribal culture. They are being ruled by non-tribals. Consequently, the tribal system is being effectively observed in their society. As in the past so also in the present, tribals are looked down upon and labelled as backward, uncivilised and stupid. They are unable to keep abreast of the progress of civilisation. They seem to be at a crossroads of civilisation, unable to decide whether to hold on to their age-old traditions or follow the mainstream of civilisation. The theological task here would be to make tribals a progressive community without cutting and weakening their culture. Only then they can remove their weaknesses, such as lack of work-culture, easy-going life, addiction to drink and lack of high aims and determination to achieve them at all costs. If they could work in these areas to improve their conditions, they would be able to stand on an equal footing with others.[24]

Here are a few practical suggestions about tribalisation in favour of Indian tribals:

* Retention of historical human identities against assimilation

---

[23] Cf. M. Bhuria, *Adivasikaran: Tribalisation and Aborignalisation,* 18.

[24] Cf. P. Kullu, "Theology in Tribal Religio-Cultural Context," in *Sevartham,* 28 (2003), 79.

- Preservation, promotion, innovation and integration of the cultural heritage of tribals

- Revival of indigenousness in order to protect human, social and cultural identity

- Protection of human and minority rights and all other resources

- Introduction of qualitative education and promotion of indigenous talents to the highest level

- Inculcation of acceptance of one's social status as creation of God.

Tribal Identity and Mission

We have already seen the tension between Christian tribals and non-Christian tribals in India due to the difference in the advancement in society. Missionaries should also reassure by word and deed that the tribal world view and the core values of tribal culture will not be replaced by other world views and values, but respected and preserved among the Christian members. Thus, it will avoid intra-tribal tensions and the rise of anti-Christian revival movements.[25]

---

[25] Cf. S. Karotemprel, "The Indigenous/Tribal Peoples and a Renewed Church in Asia," 12. The ideal way in maintaining the tribal identity during the missionary Evangelisation is exposed by Peter Tete: "The activities of the missionaries through the preaching of Christianity and education made a deep impact on the socio-economic conditions, culture and religion of the Tribals. . . One notices that the tribal population of Chotanagpur, a whole, accepted Christianity without abandoning its tribal identity" (P. Tete, "The Christian Mission and Tribal Identity," 43).

It is a fact that tribal culture and tribal religious belief are inseparably related. Tribals consider that their culture (way of life) is willed, taught and dictated by God. According to the tribal cognitive world, culture is defined as the expression of beliefs, or beliefs concretised in human actions. Therefore, faithfulness to their traditional culture would mean faithfulness to God.[26] So a total abandonment of their cultural identity in order to accept another religion would be wounding tribals in general, resulting in anti-conversion movements by the rest of the group—the present problem in India. At the same time, in the encounter with Jesus Christ, certain changes in the attitude and way of life are sure to happen. Now a safe and sound principle would be the incarnational approach of Jesus whereby he took on human nature, was born and lived in a culture, but without sin. A missionary can, in this way (other than sinful elements), adopt all the positive elements of tribal culture and help tribals in maintaining them.

The Church's task includes helping people to preserve and express their identity in the face of modernisation, urbanisation and exploitation and keeping alive and promoting their cultural traditions. The Church must undertake dialogue with the followers of traditional religions in order to reaffirm the positive human and divine values expressed in them and to lay sound bases for cooperation and solidarity with the followers of traditional religions. At the same time, the Church must defend the right of indigenous or tribal peoples to become Christ's disciples without being thereby cut off from their ancestral roots.[27]

---

[26] Cf. P. Kullu, "Tribal Culture and its Importance for Liturgy, Catechesis and Biblical Apostolate," 51.

[27] Cf. FABC, "Message of the FABC consultation on "Indigenous /Tribal Peoples in Asia and the Challenges of the Future",

In the process of inculturation, we have to be actively aware of the presence of very precious positive values that are enshrined in the ethos and the geniuses of our indigenous peoples. In particular, our people have a strong sense of community and solidarity that is threatened by materialism, consumerism and the accompanying spirit of individualism. In the dialogue with the Church, this sense of community grows into a more universal outreach beyond the boundaries of tribe or clan. Another element that needs to be respected is the strong bond that indigenous peoples have with land, forest and nature in general.[28]

> The outrageous technocratic paradigm of development, modernization syndrome, money economy, doctrine of individualism etc., has cut at the very roots of tribal vision of life and cultural values. They are made to feel inferior in matters of their own lifestyle, dance, dress, house, art, customs and folklore, their history disdained, and their language, religion and culture are severely impaired and stigmatized. This is a cultural ethnocide.[29]

(Pattaya, Thailand, 18 December 2001) in M. D. Saturnino (ed), *Indigenous Peoples in Asia and Challenges of the Future*, 187. Ethnicity, ethnic territory and political power have recently become very crucial components of shaping Tribal identity in India. Many groups prefer to be recognized and addressed by Tribal names rather than simply as the officially designated "Scheduled Tribe". This shows how important an ethnic name is to Tribal people. The demands and desires for ethnic territories are closely linked with Tribal identity. The importance of political power for establishing and shaping the Tribal identity is also a very crucial issue today (D. L. Touthang, "Tribal Identity and Contemporary Christian Mission in India," 5).

[28] Cf. D. Jala, "What the Church can do with/for Indigenous Peoples," 51.

[29] I. U. B. Reddy, "Impact of Industrialization on Tribal Life," in *Social Change*, 23 (1993), 65-66. Cited in M. G. Kariapuram, "Government Policy Towards the Tribals and Tribal Alienation in India," in *Indian Missiological Review*, 19, 3 (1996), 31; D. Jala, "What the Church can do with/for Indigenous peoples," 51.

In the last few years, there has been an identity crisis amongst Indian tribals. In the past, religion and culture were crucial elements for maintaining tribal identity. Today, the questions of land, ethnicity, ethnic territory and political power have become important issues for tribal identity in India. In the past, Christian mission was successful in giving a new interpretation to tribal religion and culture in such a way that their identity was strengthened and crystallised by Christianity. Today, contemporary Christian mission needs to offer a Christian framework and interpretation on land, ethnicity, ethnic territory and political power.[30] There is a danger that if contemporary Christian mission does not provide the framework for thought and action on these issues, the tribals of India will look to other quarters, which may be totally opposed to Christian faith and teaching.

There is a need of certain strategies and principles to be followed by contemporary Christian missions working among the tribals so that meaningful integration of tribal culture into the Christian faith can take place.[31] This can also avoid the allegations of detribalisation against Christian missionaries; in the words of D. L. Touthang:

> Christian faith must be presented in the ideology, language, idioms, traditions and history of the Tribal society so that Christianity is indigenized and contextualized to Tribal situation rather than Christianity taking the Tribals away from their context. There is a

---

[30] Cf. D. L. Touthang, "Tribal Identity and Contemporary Christian Mission in India," 6.

[31] On the one hand missionaries must enter into the local cultures, adopting all the genuine values of the culture; one the other, the mentality and cultural expressions must be evangelised" (J. Dinh Duc Dao, "Evangelisation and Culture in Asia: Problems and Prospects," 76).

need for recognition and appreciation of Tribal life and
culture. The commonalties between Tribal life and
Christian faith need to be recognized. In this way,
Christianity will be able to be presented as the fulfilment
of Tribal aspirations and longings.[32]

Christ needs to be identified in the tribal culture, in their tribal
beliefs, myths, sacrifices, historical events, personalities, etc.
Such an approach will make indigenous and Christian beliefs
interact in such a way that they will enrich one another. Then
Christianity in India will no longer look foreign. Secondly,
tribals of India will not feel uprooted and alienated from their
cultures. This approach will, at the same time, bring faith
and life closer to each other. Faith will then not remain just
a mental concept, but will be expressed in the day-to-day lives
of people.[33]

---

[32] D. L. Touthang, "Tribal Identity and Contemporary Christian
Mission in India," 6.

[33] Cf. P. Kullu, "Tribal Culture and its Importance for Liturgy,
Catechesis and Biblical Apostolate," in *Word and Worship*, 26, 2
(1993), 115.

CHAPTER 7

Priorities in Primacy of Proclamation

As a Persian saying goes, religion is like a candle. It can light up the cottage as well as burn the cottage down. More often it is used to burn the cottage down rather than light it up. That is very true of the situation in India. But then we should not get intimidated and stop the proclamation of the Gospel. First and foremost, the Church should do some soul-searching regarding its activities and style of functioning.[1] Primacy of proclamation is based on the missionary command of Jesus: "Go . . . make disciples, baptise, teach" (Mt. 28:18-20); "preach to every creature" (Mk. 16:15); Jesus gives a commission (Lk. 24: 47-48); "As the Father has sent me I am sending you" (Jn. 20:21). Jesus had foreseen persecutions for the missionaries and gave necessary instructions about this while he sent his disciples to preach the Gospel (Mt. 10:16-25; Lk.10:3). Therefore, trials and tribulations should not cause the missionaries to turn back from the missionary commitment, but rather strengthen it by the joy of witnessing the Gospel. The Gospel proclamation cannot exist without a life witness. Witness requires

---

[1] Cf. A. Poruthur, "Contemporary Challenges for Mission in North India," 366.

proclamation: "This Jesus God raised up, and of that we are all witnesses" (Acts. 2:32).

It is good to recall the words of the two great missionaries of all times: St. Peter (along with St. John) says: "We cannot but speak of what we have seen and heard" (Acts. 4:20), and St. Paul states emphatically: "Woe to me if I do not preach the Gospel" (1Cor. 9:16). Pope John Paul considered that evangelisation is "the primary service which the Church can render to every individual and to all humanity in the modern world."[2] For the Pontiff, faith was the most precious pearl to be shared: "The Church's faith in Jesus is a gift received and a gift to be shared; it is the greatest gift which the Church can offer to Asia."[3]

Primacy of Proclamation as Commitment

The Second Vatican Council taught clearly that the entire Church is missionary and that the work of evangelisation is the duty of the whole People of God.[4] The Magisterium since then has repeatedly stressed the primacy of the proclamation of Jesus in all evangelising work. Thus, Pope Paul VI explicitly wrote that "there is no true evangelisation if the name, the teaching, the life, the promises, the Kingdom and the mystery of Jesus of Nazareth, the Son of God, are not proclaimed."[5] Pope John Paul II in *Ecclesia in Asia* seems to give an overall primacy to proclamation as compared to other elements of the evangelising mission. On the significance and inevitable primacy of explicit proclamation he says, "There can be no true evangelisation without the explicit proclamation of Jesus as our Lord."[6]

---

[2] RM 2.
[3] EA 10.
[4] Cf. EA 42; cf. AG 2, 35.
[5] EN 22: *AAS* 68 (1976), 20; EA 19.
[6] EA 19.

Primacy of proclamation comes under obedience to Christ's command and it is the duty of every Christian, especially all those who are called to proclamation and evangelisation. "This insistence on proclamation is prompted not by sectarian impulse or the spirit of proselytism nor any sense of superiority. The Church evangelises in obedience to Christ's command, in the knowledge that every person has the right to hear the Good News of the God who reveals and gives himself in Christ."[7]

The present situation for evangelisation among tribals in India is not so favourable for putting into practice the teachings of the Church as it may be in other parts of the world. These difficulties are general phenomena for evangelisation in Asia. These kinds of difficulties were foreseen by Asian Bishops years ago and referred to the official Church and reflected in the Apostolic letter *Ecclesia in Asia.*

> Yet even during the consultations before the Synod many Asian Bishops referred to *difficulties in proclaiming Jesus as the only Saviour.* During the Assembly, the situation was described in this way: "Some of the followers of the great religions of Asia have no problem in accepting Jesus as a manifestation of the Divine or the Absolute, or as an 'enlightened one'. But it is difficult for them to see Him as the only manifestation of the Divine.[8]

The evangeliser is committed to proclamation, inter-religious dialogue and liberation. There is no question of ignoring proclamation. Similarly inviting people to become Christ's disciples in the Church is part of our commitment.[9] Preaching the Word of God is necessary "but this preaching must be

---

[7] EA 20; Cf. RM 46: *AAS* 83 (1991), 292f.

[8] EA 20.

[9] Cf. D. Bhatt, "Evangelisation in the Context of Hindu Culture and Religion of North India," 351.

situated in the life of a community so that men are prepared to understand it and can respond to it."[10]

The Church cannot renege on her duty to proclaim Jesus Christ, which is her fundamental duty. Respect for religions and cultures do not eliminate this need to explicitly proclaim the Gospel in its fullness.[11] This duty also implies the sharing aspect of the God-given gift to each and every one with a specific purpose. The Church's faith in Jesus is a gift received and a gift to be shared; it is the greatest gift that the Church can offer to Asia. Sharing the truth of Jesus Christ with others is the solemn duty of all who have received the gift of faith. In the Encyclical Letter *Redemptoris Missio* and later in *Ecclesia in Asia*, John Paul II exhorted:

> The Church, and every individual Christian within her, may not keep hidden or monopolize this newness and richness which has been received from God's bounty in order to be communicated to all mankind... Those who are incorporated in the Catholic Church ought to sense their privilege and for that very reason their greater obligation of *bearing witness to the faith and to the Christian life* as a service to their brothers and sisters and as a fitting response to God.[12]

Primacy of Proclamation to Tribals

In Chapter 1 of EA, while presenting the Asian context and referring to world's major religions, the encyclical mentioned: "Millions also espouse traditional or tribal religions, with varying degrees of structured ritual and formal religious teaching. The Church has the deepest respect for these

---

[10] D. S. Amalorpovadass, *The Theology of Indirect Evangelisation*, 16.

[11] Cf. D. Jala, "What the Church can do with/for Indigenous Peoples", 49; EA 19.

[12] RM 11; EA 10.

traditions and seeks to engage in sincere dialogue with their followers. The religious values they teach await their fulfilment in Jesus Christ."[13] This document accepted the existence of traditional religions and expressed the Church's concern and respect for them. The document continues this aspect repeatedly, "There are also millions of indigenous or tribal people throughout Asia living in social, cultural and political isolation from the dominant population."[14]

In India, according to the 2001 Census, tribal populations account for about 84.32 million, constituting 8.2 per cent of India's total population.[15] A significant number of tribals have accepted the Gospel message, and they still continue to do so. So, it is important to examine the Church's missionary commitment to the indigenous people of India and the areas of renewal.[16] Very often it is among the tribals that the Christian missionary finds warmer welcome and closer fellowship than among the highly established Hindu societies.[17]

The priority of proclamation among the tribals was discussed as an important theme in the seventh plenary assembly of FABC in Thailand (1995). In the paper presented by Sebastian Karotemprel, there was a statement:

> Tens of millions of Indigenous/Tribal peoples all over Asia have yet to receive the first proclamation about salvation in Jesus Christ and his Church. All local Churches must give priority to *missio ad gentes* among Indigenous/Tribal

---

[13] EA 6.

[14] *Ibid.*, 7.

[15] Cf. http://www.indiabudget.nic.in, "Social Sectors," 243.

[16] Cf. S. Karotemprel, "The Indigenous/Tribal peoples and a Renewed Church in Asia," 1.

[17] V. F. Vineeth, "Theological Formation in the North Indian Context of Religious Pluralism," 31.

peoples, since they, more than others, give a positive response to the Gospel message of salvation in Jesus Christ. It means that local Churches in Asia must release more resources and personnel for evangelisation work among the Indigenous/Tribal peoples of their regions or countries.[18]

Proclamation, which respects the rights of consciences, does not violate freedom, since faith always demands a free response on the part of the individual.[19] Respect, however, does not eliminate the need for the explicit proclamation of the Gospel in its fullness. Especially in the context of the rich array of cultures and religions in Asia, it must be pointed out that "neither respect and esteem for these religions nor the complexity of the questions raised are an invitation to the Church to withhold from these non-Christians the proclamation of Jesus Christ."[20]

Among the tribals, proclamation can be presenting Jesus Christ as the liberator. In the midst of the economic and social problems of tribals, they need a helping hand to liberate them from their miseries. This has to be achieved through prophetic witness and liberating activities of Christian missionaries, which requires the necessity of involvement in the struggles of tribal people and liberating them from their miseries. This aspect of tribal mission is reflected in *Ecclesia in Asia*:

> In almost every Asian country, there are large aboriginal populations, some of them on the lowest economic rung... Herein lies an immense field of action in education and health care, as well as in promoting social participation. The Catholic community needs to intensify pastoral work

---

[18] S. Karotemprel, "The Indigenous/Tribal peoples and a Renewed Church in Asia," 14.

[19] Cf. RM 39: *AAS* 83 (1991), 287; EA 20.

[20] EN 53: *AAS* 68 (1976), 41f; EA 20.

among these people, attending to their concerns and to the questions of justice which affect their lives. This implies an attitude of deep respect for their traditional religion and its values; it implies as well the need to help them to help themselves, so that they can work to improve their situation and become the evangelisers of their own culture and society.[21]

This prime duty of the church among all peoples to proclaim Jesus as Saviour of all is of special significance for Indian tribal populations who are, in a special way, open to the message of Christ. This character of openness to the Word of God is recognised as a common feature of all indigenous people:

> Peoples of Indigenous/Tribal origin have world views and values that are similar to Biblical world views and values. They are, therefore, open to the work of evangelisation, especially as *missio ad gentes*.[22]

Proclamation with Renewed Spirit and Courage

We must learn lessons from the past and beware of the current moves against evangelisation, the possible danger that these can bring unless certain changes in the methods are brought into the present system. The present way of inculturation in India is not sufficient to avoid attacks from the fundamentalists.[23] The recent attacks on Christians and Christian institutions in Orissa, Karnataka, Madhya Pradesh and Kerala should be treated as an eye-opener for the Church.

---

[21] EA 34.

[22] S. Karotemprel, "The Indigenous /Tribal Peoples and a Renewed Church in Asia," 14. The number of Indigenous people in Asia also gives us the understanding about this fertile soil for Word of God: "The largest single minority of Asia's Christianity is Indigenous" (*ibid.*).

[23] According to A. Poruthur, "Three decades ago religious sisters took to wearing saffron saris in place of habits as clear sign of identifying with Indian culture. Some cosmetic changes

Therefore, introspection is required with re-evaluation of the past and necessary reformation in the present methods of evangelisation:

> The issues we face and the events that have taken place, must help us to do deeper introspection about what we believe, what we teach and the methods we adopt, the terminology we use, etc. We also need to re-examine the Church structures, our way of functioning, our financial investments, the way we use our human resource potential. In the area of media, we need to consolidate and network our fragmented efforts to bring to everyone a clear picture of the issues involved.[24]

Most of the Church personnel are naive in their understanding of the situation in the country. According to them, attacks on missionaries will not last long. The Church's activities in the area of education and social work will be allowed to continue; what we are experiencing now is only a passing phase. This is an over-optimistic view and it seems to be based on what is being proclaimed as the public face of Hinduism—that it is a tolerant religion. But the recent series of attacks unleashed on Christians should make them sit up and think hard of its implications for the future.[25]

---

were also introduced into the liturgy like performing *arati*, donning *tilak* on the forehead, etc. Alas, the bitter truth is one has written a thesis on Krishn and Christ or 'shankara and Thomas Aquinas', or 'Geetha and Gospel' whether one is practicing Kundalini yoga or transcendental meditation, it all makes no difference for the fundamentalist. They are busy with their definite anti-minority plans" (A. Poruthur, "Contemporary Challenges for Mission in North India," 360-361).

[24] G. Plathottam, "Religious Fundamentalism, Media Blitzkrieg and Our Response," 36.

[25] Cf. A. Poruthur, "Contemporary Challenges for Mission in North India," 365.

The methodology used for proclamation in other parts of the world cannot be applied to the Indian tribal situation. We have to discover a method of proclamation suited to the indigenous people of North India, with official Church support.

> The presentation of Jesus Christ as the only Saviour needs to follow a *pedagogy* which will introduce people step by step to the full appropriation of the mystery. Clearly, the initial evangelisation of non-Christians and the continuing proclamation of Jesus to believers will have to be different in their approach. In initial proclamation, for example, 'the presentation of Jesus Christ could come as the fulfilment of the yearnings expressed in the mythologies and folklore of the Asian peoples'. In general, narrative methods akin to Asian cultural forms are to be preferred. In fact, the proclamation of Jesus Christ can most effectively be made by narrating his story, as the Gospels do.[26]

The lifestyle of missionaries has also a great role to play in better evangelisation. Following the incarnational approach of Jesus, missionaries have to choose a lifestyle without projecting that they are foreigners to the culture. Unless a missionary can come down to the level of the people to be evangelised, in the aspects of material commodities and simplicity of life, it is difficult to get a good result. For this "poverty in spirit" alone would not do; external poverty is also necessary, which can be understood by the people.

In the midst of communal violence, spiritual renewal is the need of the hour. In the light of the violent and pathological turn that the communal situation in our country is taking, one would venture to suggest the need for re-thinking our ideas of mission. India has been a crucible of religions. Our experiences of religious and cultural plurality

---

[26] EA 20.

are vast, rich and unique. But the needs of our times call us to go further than that. We need to become a crucible of spirituality.[27]

> Today we suffer simultaneously from the floods of fanatical religiosity and a devastating drought in spirituality. Our meagre spiritual capital is being squandered in the ruthless chase for material gains and political power. The need of the hour is not the conversion of the individual. It is the transformation of the society as a whole. Nothing less than the spiritual renewal of all religions will do for this purpose. And, given the resources of biblical spirituality, the Christian community should be equipped to serve as a catalyst for this mega spiritual ferment, despite our numerical disadvantages.[28]

Atrocities against the Church should in no way make us idle with regard to missionary commitment and proclamation. Instead, those matters should strengthen our missionary zeal, enabling us to face the next millennium with courage and confidence. Service to the needy as well as the missionary's efforts to build peace, reconciliation and harmony among all categories of people should continue uninterrupted.[29]

To proclaim Christ in the midst of violence against Christian missionaries and faithful in India is a difficult and challenging task. Therefore, in the present context, evangelisation among the tribal population of North India

---

[27] Cf. V. Thampu, "Mission and the Fundamentalist Challenge," in *Mission Today*, 2 (2000), 31-32. "Holiness must be called a fundamental presupposition and an irreplaceable condition for everyone in fulfilling the mission of salvation in the Church" (RM 90).

[28] V. Thampu, "Mission and the Fundamentalist Challenge," 31-32.

[29] Cf. G. Plathottam, "Religious Fundamentalism, Media Blitzkrieg and Our Response," 37.

needs special courage and strength, which could only be acquired from the Holy Spirit. A missionary should even be ready to face martyrdom in fulfilling the commitment to the missionary command of Jesus. John Paul II, in his encyclical, *Veritatis Splendor*, dedicated a section to martyrdom. He writes: "Martyrdom is an outstanding sign of the holiness of the Church. Fidelity to God's law, witnessed to by death, is a solemn proclamation and missionary commitment."[30] The early Christians considered martyrdom as a supreme witness to Christ and an expression of their radical following of Christ (cf. Acts. 7:54-60; 12:1-2). In the midst of persecution and suffering, the task of missionaries is to move forward with unshakeable faith and hope in Jesus. Missionaries must never lose hope in the prophetic word of the Spirit. The prophetic and protective voice of Jesus, 'Fear not, I am with you' (cf. Lk. 12:1-12), has to be heard every time.

⊂〇⊃

---

[30] John Paul II, Encyclical Letter *Veritatis Splendor* (6 August 1993), 93.

Conclusion

A deeper delving into the base of the religion and culture of indigenous people can enlighten us about the many positive elements with very good fertility and atmosphere for the germination and growth of the seed: 'The Word of God'—the Gospel message. The additional preparation of the ground, facilitating sowing the new 'seed' requires careful understanding of the vulnerability of the local situation. In tribal religion, there are various elements favouring evangelisation but those elements require a kind of purification at the level of Christian faith and practices. What we need to do is evangelise tribal culture through a contextual approach instead of 'taking them out of their traditional culture,' which would create accusation from onlookers, especially fanatics of other faiths in the region. The Word has to be incarnated in the geographical-historical, socio-political and cultural background of local tribes.

At present, there are many challenges for evangelisation in India. Challenges from Hindu fundamentalist organisations are the greatest of the challenges that evangelisation among tribals faces today. The conversion issue spread out like a flame panicking the evangelisation in North India. But census figures reveal that the accusations against Christian missionaries do not hold water, as there has been no remarkable increase in the number of Christians in India. There are occasional attacks on Christian institutions and individuals creating terror, blocking the activities of Christian missionaries. This phenomenon still continues in different parts of India. These attacks from Hindu fundamentalist organisations seem to be politically motivated, as the attacking organisations are connected to political parties and attacks on Christians normally increase before public elections. Besides, these Hindu fundamentalist organisations carry out a so-called re-conversion process with violence, forcibly reconverting Christian tribals to Hinduism.

Another external challenge is the accusation of detribalisation. It is widely noticed that the cultural difference between Christian tribals and non-Christian tribals is totally blamed on Christian missionaries. There are remarkable changes among Christian tribals from their original indigenous culture in various dimensions; in lifestyle affecting tribal unity and solidarity and in art and language. At the same time, the influence of Christian missionaries on improving the living standards of tribals through education cannot be enlisted as negative remarks even though there is change from traditional lifestyle.

Apart from external challenges there are internal challenges as well; they appear because of incongruity of missionaries in the locality of evangelisation. Insufficiency of deep-rootedness in local culture and in one's own faith is one of the major challenges faced by Christian missionaries. Knowingly or unknowingly, the Church in India is projecting western culture in various ways, such as construction of buildings, art, life-style of missionaries, language, etc. This projection erodes deep rootedness in local culture and ends up being a deviation from Jesus' incarnation approach. This phenomenon is seen as caused by defects in the formation of missionaries. During formation, a candidate has to be well equipped with the knowledge and experience of the local culture of his or her future mission. Again, this situation is intensified due to the inefficiency of incarnated and solidarity-forwarded movement in the struggles of tribals for liberating mission.

Proposed Priorities for Evangelisation Among Tribals of North India

The above challenges lead to proposing a few priorities for contemporary evangelisation among the indigenous people of North India. Priority in formation of missionaries is the first one put forward in this work. Missionaries who are intending to do ministry among North Indian tribals should be re-oriented with sufficient knowledge of the local culture and life-situation of the people. They should be encouraged to take an interest in coming down and living among the people and do evangelisation by using the incarnation method of Jesus. Also, encouragement should be given to local tribals to come out for evangelisation so that they can get comparatively more success because of their acquaintance with the local culture. This encouragement for local vocations has to include both consecrated life and lay apostolate. Contextual theology has to be given importance in formation houses. In relation with tribal areas, tribal theology has to be developed and be given due importance in formation houses. This contextual theological formation may strengthen missionaries to become competent ministers and do better service among the indigenous people of North India.

Priorities in witnessing to Gospel values are indispensable for evangelisation. The first form of witness is the very life of the missionary and an irreplaceable form of mission. People are persuaded more by holiness of life than by intellectual argument, and expression in a witness of life speaks the Gospel eloquently. Prophetic witness is the second form of witness that has been dealt with in this book. People of today demand a heroic witnessing from missionaries. Missionaries have to support the cause of tribals who seek a just and equitable recognition of their identity and rights. They need to help them especially in getting a just solution to the complex quest of the alienation of their lands. Tribals groan for liberation from the evils that have rocked the very foundations of their society. The third kind of witness proposed is witnessing of charity. Charity and the mission of preaching go hand in hand. Charitable services, especially educational charity, play an important and supportive role in the evangelistic work going on amongst the poor tribals. All charitable services function as an entry point for Christian workers to share God's love with the indigenous people of North India.

In the present situation, priorities regarding inter-religious and cultural aspects have to be taken into account for better evangelisation among tribals. In the midst of various threats from fundamentalism and religious fanatics, a missionary has to give priority to having healthy relation with existing local religious leaders and leaders of fundamentalist religious organisations. Inter-religious dialogue and inculturation may be some of the means of having healthy relations with the members of other religions. In tribal mission, it is not Hindu culture but tribal culture that has to be given importance for inculturation. Promotion of tribal culture through tribalisation movements can be a safe way in the midst of the accusations that missionaries are doing detribalisation and the Hinduisation process of Hindu fundamentalist organisations. Preservation, promotion, innovation and integration of the cultural heritage of tribals should be considered as priorities. Missionaries should also reassure by word and deed that the tribal world view and the core values of tribal culture will not be replaced by other world views and values, but respected and preserved among Christian members. Incarnating the Gospel in people's cultures is the need of the time. Missionaries who come from other cultures and countries must immerse themselves in the cultural milieu of tribals—to whom they are sent.

Evangelisation is the duty of the People of God, and recent Church teachings have repeatedly stressed the primacy of the proclamation of Jesus Christ. The evangeliser is committed to proclamation, inter-religious dialogue and liberation. There is no question of ignoring proclamation, even in the midst of the persecutions that are seen in India. This prime duty of the Church among all peoples to proclaim Jesus as Saviour of all is of special significance for Indian tribal populations who are, in a special way, open to the message of Christ. The priority of proclamation among tribals was discussed as an important theme in the seventh plenary assembly of the FABC in Thailand (1995). Missionaries have to discover a method of proclamation that suits the indigenous people of India. In the midst of communal violence, spiritual renewal is the need of the hour. Atrocities against the Church should strengthen our missionary zeal and encourage us to face the next millennium with courage and confidence.

The Author's Encounter with Pope Benedict XVI during the Annual meeting of Roman Clergy[1]

Dialogue and Mission

Fr. Paul Chungat, parochial Vicar of San Giuseppe Cottolengo: My name is Fr. Chungat, I am Indian. I am temporarily parochial vicar of San Giuseppe, Valle Aurelia. I would like to thank you for the opportunity you have given me to serve for three years in the diocese of Rome. It has been a great help to me for my studies, as I believe it is for all student priests who stay on in Rome. The time has now come for me to return to my diocese in India, where Catholics account for only 1 per cent, whereas 99 per cent are non–Christians. What has given me much food for thought in the past few days is the situation of missionary evangelisation in my Homeland. In the recent Note of the Congregation of the Doctrine of the Faith there are several words that are not easy to understand in the context of interreligious dialogue. For example, in n.10, "Fullness of

---

[1] "The Holy Father meets with the clergy of Rome, 7 February", *Osservatore Romano*, 20 February 2008, p. 8-9.

salvation", and in the Introduction, "the need for formal incorporation in the Church." These are concepts that it will be difficult to make people understand when I take these things back to India, where I will have to talk to my Hindu friends and to the faithful of other religions. My question is: Should "fullness of salvation" be understood in a qualitative or a quantitative sense? In a quantitative sense, it is somewhat difficult. The Second Vatican Council tells us that it is also possible to find a ray of light in other faiths. In a qualitative sense, in addition to the historicity and fullness of the faith, what other things show the oneness of our faith in the context of interreligious dialogue?

Pope Benedict XVI: Thank you for your presentation. You know well that the breadth of your questions would require a semester of theology! I shall try to be brief. You know theology, there are great teachers and many books.

First of all, thank you for your testimony, for you say you are glad to be able to work in Rome although you are Indian. I find this a marvelous phenomenon of catholicity. Today, not only do missionaries from the West go to other continents, but there is an exchange of gifts: Indians, Africans, and South Americans work with us and our people go to other continents. There is giving and receiving on all sides; precisely this accounts for the vitality of catholicity, where we are all indebted to the gifts of the Lord and are then able to give them to one another.

It is in this reciprocity of gifts, of giving and receiving, that the Catholic Church lives. You can learn from these Western environments and experiences and we in turn can learn. I see that this religious spirit which exists in Asia, as in Africa, surprises European whose faith is all too often somewhat cool.

This vivacity, at least of the religious spirit that exists on these continents, is consequently a great gift to all of us, especially to us Bishops of the Western world and in particular of those countries where the phenomenon of immigration is more pronounced, from the Philippines, from India, etc. Our cold Catholicism is revived by this fervor that comes from you. Hence, catholicity is a great gift.

Let us come to the questions you have put to me. I do not have here before me the exact words of the Document of the Congregation for the Doctrine of the Faith to which you referred, but in any case I would like to say two things.

On the one hand, dialogue, mutual knowledge, mutual respect and the effort for all possible forms of collaboration for the great purpose of humanity or for important needs in order to overcome fanaticism and create a spirit of peace and love are absolutely necessary.

This is also in the spirit of the Gospel, whose meaning is precisely that the spirit of love which we learned from Jesus, the peace of Jesus which he gave to us through the Cross, may become universally present in the world. In this sense dialogue must be true dialogue with respect for others and with the acceptance of their otherness; yet it must also be evangelical, in the sense that its fundamental purpose is to help people live in love and ensure that this love is extended in every part of the world.

But this most necessary dimension of dialogue, that is, respect for the other, tolerance, co-operation, does not exclude the other dimension: the fact that the Gospel is a great gift, the gift of great love, of great truth, which we cannot only keep to ourselves alone. We must offer it to others, realising that God gives them the necessary freedom and light to find the truth. This is the truth.

And so I too am taking this road. Mission is not imposition but offering God's gift, allowing his goodness to enlighten people so that the gift of actual friendship with God with a human face may be extended.

We therefore want and must always witness to this faith and love that are inherent in our faith. Had we left others on their own and kept the faith we have just for ourselves, we would have neglected a true human and divine duty. We would also be unfaithful to ourselves were we not to offer this faith to the world, even while always respecting the freedom of others. The presence of faith in the world is a positive element, even if it does not convert anyone; it is a reference point.

Exponents of non-Christian religions have said to me: the presence of Christianity is a reference point for us that helps us, even if we do not convert.

Let us think of the great figure of Mahatma Gandhi; although he remained firmly bound to his own religion, the Sermon on the Mount was a fundamental reference point for him, which shaped his whole life. Thus, the leaven of faith, even if it did not convert him to Christianity, entered his life.

It seems to me that this leaven of Christian love which flows from the Gospel – in addition to missionary work that seeks to enlarge the spaces of faith – is a service we render to humanity.

Let us think of St. Paul. I recently examined his missionary motivation. I also spoke of it to the Curia at our end of the year meeting. Paul was moved by the Lord's word in his eschatological discourse. Before any other event, before the return of the Son of Man, the Gospel must be preached to all peoples. A condition for the world to attain perfection, for it to be open to Heaven, is that the Gospel be proclaimed to all.

He devoted all his missionary zeal to ensuring that the Gospel reached everyone, possibly already in his generation, in response to the Lord's command "so that it may be announced to all the peoples." His desire was not so much to baptise all peoples as rather that the Gospel, hence, the fulfillment of history as such, be present in the world.

I think that by looking at history's progress it is possible today to understand better that this presence of the Word of God, this proclamation which, like leaven, reaches everyone, is necessary in order that the word truly achieves its goal. In this sense, we indeed desire the conversion of all but allow the Lord to be the one who acts.

What is important is that those who wish to convert have the possibility to do so and that the Lord's light appears over the world as a reference point for everyone and a light that helps, without which the world cannot find itself. I do not know whether I have explained myself properly: not only do dialogue and mission not exclude each other, but they also help each other.

Bibliography

I. CHURCH'S MAGISTERIUM[1]

1. Documents of Vatican Council II

Optatam Totius, Decree on the Priestly Formation, (28 October 1965), in *AAS* 58 (1966), 713-727.

Ad Gentes Divinitus, Decree on the Church's missionary activity (7 December 1965), in *AAS* 58 (1966) 947-990.

Presbyterorum Ordinis, Decree on the Ministry and Life of Priests (7 December 1965), in *AAS* 58 (1966) 991-1024.

2. Papal Documents

Paul VI, "Homily during Mass at Stadium, Djakarta," (3 December 1970), in *AAS* 63, 1971, 76-81.

__________, "Message for Mission Sunday," (21 October 1973), in *The Teachings of Paul VI*, Libreria Editrice Vaticana, Vatican City 1973, 299.

__________, "Address to the Members of the *consilium de laicis*" (2 October 1974), in *AAS* 66 (1974), 567-570.

__________, Apostolic Exhortation *Evangelii Nuntiandi* (8 December 1975), in *AAS* 68 (1976) 5-76.

---

[1] Here we have given the documents in chronological order. The English translation of the Counciliar and Post-Counciliar documents is taken from Flannery A. (ed.), *Vatican Council II: The Counciliar and Post Counciliar Documents*, St. Paul's Publications, Bombay 1989.

John Paul II, Encyclical Letter *Redemptoris Missio* (8 December 1990), in *AAS* 83 (1991) 249-340, English Version: St. Paul Publications, Boston 1986.

__________, Encyclical Letter *Veritatis Splendor* (6 August 1993), in *AAS* 85 (1993)1133-1228, English Version: Libreria Editrice Vaticana, Vatican 1993,

__________, Apostolic Exhortation *Vita Consecrata* (25 March 1996), in *AAS* 88 (1996)377-486, English Version: Libreria Editrice Vaticana, Città del Vaticano, 1996.

__________, Post-Synodal Apostolic Exhortation *Ecclesia in Asia* (6 November 1999), in *AAS* 92 (2000) 449-528.

3. Other Ecclesial Teachings, Statements and Reports

Congregation for Catholic Education, *La formazione telogica del future sacerdotale*, Rome, 1976.

Federation of Asian Bishop's Conference, "Recommendations of the Conference," in *Evangelisation among the Indigenous Peoples of Asia: A Report of a Conference on the Concerns of Indigenous Peoples Hua Hin, Thailand, September 3-8, 1995*, FABC Papers, no. 80, 92g.

__________, "Message of the FABC consultation on "Indigenous / Tribal Peoples in Asia and the Challenges of the future," (Pattaya, Thailand, 18 December 2001) in *Indigenous Peoples in Asia and Challenges of the Future*, M. D. SATURNINO (ed.), Claretian Publications, Bangalore 2004, 187-188.

II. BOOKS AND ARTICLES

Aghamkar Atul, "Contemporary Mission Challenges in India," in *Dharma Deepika*, 9, 2 (2005), 71-80.

Amalorpavadas D. S., *The Theology of Indirect Evangelisation*, NBCLC, Bangalore 1969.

__________, *Theology of Evangelisation: in the Indian Context*, NBCLC, Bangalore 1971.

Bose Nirmal Kumar, *Culture and society in India*, Asian Publishing House, Bombay, 1967.

Bhatt Dhiranand. "Evangelisation in the Context of Hindu Culture and Religion of North India," in *Mission Today*, 7 (2005), 331-352.

Bhuria Mahipal. *Adivasikaran: Tribalisation and Aboriginalisation*, Satprakashan Press, Indore 2004.

Cabezon Antonio. "Martyrdom: The Supreme Mark of Greatness," in *Philippiniana Sacra*, 15, 44 (1980), 216-229.

Cajilig Vicente G., *Dialogue between Faith and Culture: Towards Integral Human and Social Development*, Lucky, Manila 1998.

Colaco C., *25 Years "Ad Gentes" in India*, Asian Trading Corporation, Bangalore 1991.

De Lastic Alan, "Violations of Human Rights and attack on Christians", *Supplement to Indian Currents*, 10, 48 (1998) 36.

__________, "Address at the Press Conference by the Chairman of the United Christian Forum for Human Rights on 24th November 1998," in *Supplement to Indian Currents*, 10, 48 (1998) 40-42.

Dhanabalan K. "Serving Tribal People," in *Drishtikone*, 3 (1995), 7-9.

Dinh Duc Dao Joseph, "Missiography: Present Situations and Emerging Tendencies of Mission," in *Correspondence course on Missionary Formation: Mission for the third Millenium*, Pontifical Missionary Union, Roma 1991.

__________, "La spiritualità Missionaria", in *Cristo Chiesa Missione*, Pontificia Universitas Urbaniana, Roma 1992, 386).

__________, "Present-day Situations of the Mission 'ad gentes': at the service of the poor," in *Omnis Terra* 27 [Eng. ed., 1993] 287-293.

__________, "Evangelisation and Culture in Asia: Problems and Prospects," in *Omnis Terra* 28, Eng. ed., 1994, 70-80.

__________, "Proclamation and Dialogue with the Traditional Religions of Asia and Oceania," in *Correspondence course on Missionary Formation: Mission for the third Millenium*, Pontifical Missionary Union, Roma 1997, 5.

Esquerda Bifet, Juan, "Missionary Spirituality", in *Mission for the Third Millennium*, Pontifical Mission Organization, Bangalore 1993, 297-334. 349.? Or 299

__________, *Spirituality for a Missionary Church*, Urbaniana University Press, Roma 1994.

Fernandes Walter, "Indian Tribals and the Search for an Indigenous Identity," in Social Change, xxiii, 2&3, 1993, 35-40.

Gandhi M. K., *Harijan*, 17, 4, 1937.

Gaventa Beverly Roberts, "Conversion," in D. N. FREEDMAN, *The Anchor Bible Dictionary*, Vol. 1, Doubleday, New York 1992, 1131-1133.

Golwalker M. S., *We or Our Nationhood Defined*, Bharat Prakashan, Nagpur 1938.

Hemron A. S., "Towards a Programme of Contextual and Adivasi Theology," in *Religion and Society*, 50, 3 (2005), 87-96.

Hendriks Hans, "Pastoral Pioneering Among Tribals," in *Third Millennium*, 1, 4 (1998), 64-71.

Jala Domnic, "What the Church can do with/for Indigenous Peoples," in Saturnino Dias M. (ed.), *Indigenous Peoples in Asia and Challenges of the Future*, Claretian Publications, Bangalore 2004.

Kanakappally Benedict, "Dialogue and Proclamation with Hinduism," in *Correspondence Course on Missionary Formation*, Pontifical Missionary Union – International Secretariat, Rome 1997, 3-17.

Kariapuram Mathew George, "Government Policy Towards the Tribals and Tribal Alienation in India," Indian Missiological Review, vol. 19, 3, (1996) 26-33.

Karotemprel Sebastian, "The Indigenous /Tribal peoples and a Renewed Church in Asia," in FABC Papers- No. 92g, Thailand 1995, 13

__________, "Traditional Religions," in FABC, "Recommendations of the Conference," in *Evangelisation among the Indigenous*

Peoples of Asia: A Report of a Conference on the Concerns of Indigenous Peoples Hua Hin, Thailand, September 3-8, 1995, FABC Papers: no. 80, 28-29.

Kochupurackal C., *India Awaiting the Good News,* G. M. Secretariate, Cochin 1988.

Kodithuwakku Iindunil Janakaratne, *Conversion Debate Between Buddhists and Christian in Sri Lanka Since 1990 in an Era of Globalization: A Missiological Appraisal,* Centre for Catholic Social Communication in Uva, Bandarawela 200.

Koppers Wilhelm, - JUNGBLUT Leonard, *Bowmen of Mid-India: A Monography of the Bhils of Jhabua (M.P.) and Adjoining Territories,* (vols. 1 & 2), Acta Ethnologica et Linguistica, Wien 1976.

Kullu Paulus. "Tribal Culture and its Importance for Liturgy, Catechesis and Biblical Apostolate," in *Word and Worship,* 26, 2 (1993) 5-56.

__________, "Theology in Tribal Religio-Cultural Context," in *Sevartham,* 28 (2003), 65-79.

Lakara Christopher, "Christianity and Tribal Identity," in *Religion and Society,* 34, 2 (1989), 30-39.

Le Joly Edward, *Mother Teresa: Messenger of God's Love,* St. Paul's Publications, Bombay 1988.

Lele Jayant, *Hindutva: The Emergence of the Right,* Earthworm Books, Madras 1995.

Little William –Fowler H.W. –Coulson J., "Conversion" in *The Shorter Oxford English Dictionary,* Oxford University Press, London 1944[3], 387.

Longchar A. Wati, "Tribal Theology and Theological education in India," in *National Council of Churches Review,* 121 (2001), 577-588.

__________, "Tribal Theology in the Changing Context," in *Religion and Society,* 52, 3-4 (2007), 87-97.

Madan T. N., *Modern Myths, Locked Minds: Secularism and Fundamentalism in India,* Oxford University press, New Delhi 2003.

Maheu Betty A., "A Missionary Spirituality for Asia Reflections on Ecclesia in Asia," in *Mission Today*, 2, 3 (2000), 316-322.

Manathodath Jacob, *Culture, Dialogue and the Church: A Study on the Inculturation of the Local Churches According to the Teaching of Pope Paul VI*, Intercultural publications, New Delhi 1990.

Mawrie Barnes L., "Experience of the Tribal Socio Political, Historical and Cultural Context: Quest for a Tribal Theology," in *Mission Today*, 7 (2008) 46-59.

Mehta Prakash Chandra, *Changing Face of Bhils*, Shiva Publishers, Udaipur 1998.

Michael S. M., "Real Issues Behind the Violence," in *Mission Today*, 2, (2000), 5-22.

Minj Nirmal, "Meaning of Tribal Consciousness," in *Religion and society*, 36, 2 (1989), 12-23.

__________, "Forum," in *Drishtikone*, 3 (1995), 11-13.

Minj Francis, "The Politics of Conversion: A Theological Reflection on the Current Debate on Conversion in Tribal India," in *Sevarthan*, 30 (2005), 139-157.

Moloney F. J., *Disciples and Prophets: A Biblical Model for the Religious Life*, Crossroad, New York 1981.

Mother Teresa, *A Gift for God: Prayers and Meditations*, compiled by Muggeridge M., Harper & Row, New York 1975.

__________, *One Heart Full of Love*, J. L. González – Balado (ed.), Servant Publications, Ann Arbour, Michagan 1984.

__________, *No Greater Love*, B. Benenate - J. Durepos (ed.), New World Library, Novato 1997.

Parapullil A., "Tribal Theology," in *Sevartham*, 2 (1977), 27-52.

Patel Arjun, "Hinduisation of Adivasis: A Case Study from South Gujarath," in *Dalits in Modern India: Vision and Values*, S. M. Michael (ed.), Vistaar Publications, New Delhi 1998, 186-212.

Paulose M. T., "Evangelisation in India Today," in *Sevartham*, 23 (Ranchi 1998), 113-121.

Piepke Joachim G., "Incarnation in Cultural Context," in *Indian Missiological Review*, 12, 1(1990) 39-52.

Plathottam George, "Religious Fundamentalism, Media Blitzkrieg and Our Response," in *Mission Today*, 2 (2000), 33-37.

Poruthur Anto, "Ground Realities of North Indian Mission", in *Mission Today*, 6 (Shillong 2004), 153-162.

__________, "Contemporary Challenges for Mission in North India," in *Mission Today*, 10, 4 (2008), 355-366.

Prior John Mansford, "Faith and Culture in Dialogue: A Reflective Theological Synthesis," in *Word and Worship*, 39, 5 (2006), 320-328.

Reddy I. U. B., "Impact of Industrialization on Tribal Life," in *Social Change*, 23 (1993), 65-66.

Sahu, *Tribal Culture and Identity*, Sarup & Son, New Delhi 1998.

Saldana Julian, *Inculturation*, St. Pauls Publications, Mumbai 1997.

__________, "Conversion in 'Ecclesia in Asia'," in *Mission Today*, 2, 2 (2000) 173-179.

Saraiva Martns Jose, "The Missionary Formation of Priests in the Light of the 1990 Synod and the *Pastores Dabo Vobis*," in *Mission for the Third Millennium*, Pontifical Mission Organization, Bangalore 1993, 335-361.

Scavo N., "Il cuore di Milano per i Cristiani dell'India", in *Avenire* (23 Novembre 2008), 27.

Scherer J. A. - Bevans S. B. (eds.), *New Directions in Mission and Evangelisation – 1: Basic statements 1974-1991*, Orbis Books, Mary knoll, N Y 1992.

Seunarine, J. F., *Reconversion to Hinduism through Suddhi*, The Christian Literature Society, Madras 1977.

Shouri Arun, *Harvesting Our Souls: Missionaries, Their Design, Their Claims*, ASA Publications, New Delhi, 2000.

s. n. "India Vows to Punish Christians' Murderers," in *International Herald Tribune*, Tuesday, (January 26, 1999), 6.

s. n. "In India premi dagli estremisiti indù a chi uccide cattolici", in *Avenire* (23 Novembre 2008), 3.

Srinivas M. N., *The Cohesive role of Sanskritization and Other Essays*, Oxford University Press, Delhi 1989.

Swamy T. Antony, "The Spirit of Poverty, an Essential Witness in Priestly Life in Indian Context," in *Indian Theological Studies*, 40, 3 (2003), 264-273.

Thampu V., "Mission and the Fundamentalist Challenge," in *Mission Today*, 2 (2000), 23-32.

Thazhathukunnel Joseph, "Mahatma Gandhi's Attitude to Mission," in *Ishvani Documentation and Mission Digest*, 21, 2 (2003) 204.

Tillich Paul, *Theology of Culture*, Oxford University Press, London 1959.

Tete Peter, "Christian Missions and Tribal Identity," in *Sevartham*, 24 (1999), 37-62.

Tirkey Amrit. "The Tribal Churches in India: It's identity and Challenges Today," in *Jeevadhara*, 33 (2003), 310-323.

Tirkey Justin, "Tribal Values and the Principle and Foundation," in *Sevartham*, 32 (2007), 33-46.

Touthang Dino L., "Tribal Identity and Contemporary Christian Mission in India," in *Drishtikone*, 3 (1995), 4-6.

Upreti H. C., *Indian Tribes: Then and now*, Pointer publishers, Jaipur 2007.

Valiaveetil Chacko, "Inculturation: The Need and the Scope," in *Indian Missiological Review*, 9, 1 (1987), 24-31.

Vecchia Stefano, "Orissa, il drama di mogli e madri" in *Avenire* (14 Dicembre 2008), 1,5.

Vineeth V. F., "Theological Formation in the North-Indian Context of Religious Pluralism," in *Third Millennium*, 12, 4 (2009) 28-42.

ॐ

www.ingramcontent.com/pod-product-compliance
Lightning Source LLC
Chambersburg PA
CBHW031336160726
47993CB00002B/702